IF

IF

A PLAY IN FOUR ACTS

By LORD DUNSANY

1922

DEDICATED

TO

R. A. H. PLUNKETT

FOREWORD

To praise a new play of Dunsany's is, to my
mind, like commending a sunset as a satisfac-
tory event, or expressing a favorable opinion
of the beauty of flowers. Which emphasizes
the remarkable fact that this author has no
lukewarm admirers, or temperate cavilers.
Readers of both his prose and plays divide
themselves into antithetical groups: those
who read with cool, abstract, analytical consciousness, and those who so lose themselves
in "eternal and ancient lands" that they forget language, style, the author himself, and
only when the tale is past, the play ended, do
they become again aware of the world and its
lesser affairs, remember and appreciate the
conceiver of these words and phrases, and
become conscious of some faint protest from
the wholly confused, self-controlled critics
who, like Miss Cubbidge's school-friend feel
that "it is not Proper for you to be there."

Hence any foreword such as this can be
only a very personal thing. If I were as frank

FOREWORD

as critics are supposed to be, or brief as book-reviewers ought to, or direct as a head-liner, I might sum it all up in a single sentence: I am tremendously fond of Dunsany and his work, and I am sorry for you if you're not!

The law of compensation is ever operative and those who find no thrill, no emotion of utter delight in these tales and plays, must surely draw from some other source of life's pleasure, real surfeit, of which we, his devotees, are ignorant. I have read "The Exiles' Club" probably forty times, in crowded hotel lobbies, in green and steamy jungles, in an upper berth swinging through an arc of ninety degrees, and I look forward to the forty-first reading with the certain knowledge of complete absorption. I know that the four words "I am the last" in "Charon," and the other four, "It was new then" in "The Song of the Blackbird" will seem as fresh at the next as at the first reading. There is very probably some definite reason for such un-reasoning obsession as this, but I can neither name nor phrase it. Whether Dunsany pictures little god Jabim sorrowing on a kitchen midden, or pirates sailing in a wheeled brig through the Sahara, or the men of Dales-wood scrawling their love of home in a

FOREWORD

doomed front-line trench, he compels my complete surrender of consciousness to his theme. And when such is the case, specific criticism is impossible.

Humanity overwhelmingly prefers photography to painting—the negative of a battlefield to Töten Insel, O. Henry to Maeterlinck, Conrad to Blackwood, Stevenson to Stephens. My own life, as a scientist, I find is a never-ending attempt to turn painting into photography—fairy tales into drab reality—to interpret in terms of physics, chemistry, interaction, or some sort of understandable truth, such miracles as the change from caterpillar to butterfly, the assumption of cock's plumage by a hen pheasant. While the enthusiasm of the study of bird and beast, of feeble inquiry into the evolution of life, while the joy of all this is beyond words, yet the ultimate solution, the resolving of the miracle, automatically denudes the problem of its greatest attraction, and we throw it aside and turn to the next. Two and two must surely hold more of unconscious fascination for a child, than the eternal certainty of their known sum; some of the thrill in the mysterious hieroglyphics of a gorgeous black and gold Chinese sign is lost when it is interpreted

FOREWORD

as advertising an imported hair oil. And so perhaps my sheer, uncritical joy in a play such as the "If" of the present volume, is due to the relief of leavening the dull main street of life with flowers of Carcassonne, or as in this case, with the crystal of Ali; a relief from the eternal straight line or triangle drama, which can develop or end only happily or unhappily, to a play which begins in a spirit of comedy, develops mysteriously, and ends satisfactorily.

WILLIAM BEEBE.

NEW YORK,
December 10, 1921.

IF

DRAMATIS PERSONÆ

JOHN BEAL

MARY BEAL

LIZA

ALI

BILL ⎫
BERT ⎭ *two railway porters*

THE MAN IN THE CORNER

MIRALDA CLEMENT

HAFIZ EL ALCOLAHN

DAOUD

ARCHIE BEAL

BAZZALOL ⎫
THOOTHOOBABA ⎭ *two Nubian door-keepers*

BEN HUSSEIN, *Lord of the Pass*

ZABNOOL ⎫
SHABEESH ⎭ *two conjurers*

OMAR, *a singer*

ZAGBOOLA, *mother of Hafiz*

THE SHEIK OF THE BISHAREENS

Notables, soldiers Bishareens, dancers, etc.

IF

ACT I

SCENE 1

A small railway station near London.
Time: Ten years ago.

BERT

'Ow goes it, Bill?

BILL

Goes it? 'Ow d'yer think it goes?

BERT

I don't know, Bill. 'Ow is it?

BILL

Bloody.

BERT

Why? What's wrong?

BILL

Wrong? Nothing ain't wrong.

BERT

What's up then?

IF

BILL

Nothing ain't right.

BERT

Why, wot's the worry?

BILL

Wot's the worry? They don't give you better wages nor a dog, and then they thinks they can talk at yer and talk at yer, and say wot they likes, like.

BERT

Why? You been on the carpet, Bill?

BILL

Ain't I! Proper.

BERT

Why, wot about, Bill?

BILL

Wot about? I'll tell yer. Just coz I let a lidy get into a train. That's wot about. Said I ought to 'av stopped 'er. Thought the train was moving. Thought it was dangerous. Thought I tried to murder 'er, I suppose.

BERT

Wot? The other day?

BILL

Yes.

4

IF

BERT

Tuesday?

BILL

Yes.

BERT

Why. The one that dropped her bag?

BILL

Yes. Drops 'er bag. Writes to the company. They writes back she shouldn't 'av got in. She writes back she should. Then they gets on to me. Any more of it and I'll . . .

BERT

I wouldn't, Bill; don't you.

BILL

I will.

BERT

Don't you, Bill. You've got your family to consider.

BILL

Well, anyway, I won't let any more of them passengers go jumping into trains any more, not when they're moving, I won't. When the train gets in, doors shut. That's the rule. And they'll 'ave to abide by it.

5

IF

BERT

Well, I wouldn't stop one, not if . . .

BILL

I don't care. They ain't going to 'ave me on the mat again and talk all that stuff to me. No, if someone 'as to suffer . . . 'Ere she is. . . .

[*Noise of approaching train heard.*]

BERT

Ay, that's her.

BILL

And shut goes the door.

[*Enter* JOHN BEAL.]

BERT

Wait a moment, Bill.

BILL

Not if he's . . . Not if he was *ever* so.

JOHN [*preparing to pass*]

Good morning. . . .

BILL

Can't come through. Too late.

IF

JOHN

Too late? Why, the train's only just in.

BILL

Don't care. It's the rule.

JOHN

O, nonsense. [*He carries on.*]

BILL

It's too late. I tell you you can't come.

JOHN

But that's absurd. I want to catch my train.

BILL

It's too late.

BERT

Let him go, Bill.

BILL

I'm blowed if I let him go.

JOHN

I want to catch my train.

> [JOHN *is stopped by* BILL *and pushed back by the face.* JOHN *advances towards* BILL *looking like fighting. The train has gone.*]

7

IF

BILL

Only doing my duty.

[JOHN *stops and reflects at this, deciding it isn't good enough. He shrugs his shoulders, turns round and goes away.*]

JOHN

I shouldn't be surprised if I didn't get even with you one of these days, you . . . and some way you won't expect.

Curtain

SCENE 2

Yesterday evening.

[*Curtain rises on* JOHN *and* MARY *in their suburban home.*]

JOHN

I say, dear. Don't you think we ought to plant an acacia?

MARY

An acacia, what's that, John?

JOHN

O, it's one of those trees that they have.

MARY

But why, John?

8

IF

JOHN

Well, you see the house is called The Acacias, and it seems rather silly not to have at least one.

MARY

O, I don't think that matters. Lots of places are called lots of things. Everyone does.

JOHN

Yes, but it might help the postman.

MARY

O, no, it wouldn't, dear. He wouldn't know an acacia if he saw it any more than I should.

JOHN

Quite right, Mary, you're always right. What a clever head you've got!

MARY

Have I, John? We'll plant an acacia if you like. I'll ask about it at the grocer's.

JOHN

You can't get one there.

MARY

No, but he's sure to know where it can be got.

9

IF

JOHN

Where do they grow, Mary?

MARY

I don't know, John; but I am sure they do, somewhere.

JOHN

Somehow I wish sometimes, I almost wish I could have gone abroad for a week or so to places like where acacias grow naturally.

MARY

O, would you really, John?

JOHN

No, not really. But I just think of it sometimes.

MARY

Where would you have gone?

JOHN

O, I don't know. The East or some such place. I've often heard people speak of it, and somehow it seemed so . . .

MARY

The East, John? Not the East. I don't think the East somehow is quite respectable.

JOHN

O well, it's all right, I never went, and never shall go now. It doesn't matter.

IF

MARY [*the photographs catching her eye*]

O, John, I meant to tell you. Such a dreadful thing happened.

JOHN

What, Mary?

MARY

Well, Liza was dusting the photographs, and when she came to Jane's she says she hadn't really begun to dust it, only looked at it, and it fell down, and that bit of glass is broken right out of it.

JOHN

Ask her not to look at it so hard another time.

MARY

O, what do you mean, John?

JOHN

Well, that's how she broke it; she said so, and as I know you believe in Liza . . .

MARY

Well, I can't think she'd tell a lie, John.

JOHN

No, of course not. But she mustn't look so hard another time.

11

IF

MARY

And it's poor little Jane's photograph. She will feel it so.

JOHN

O, that's all right, we'll get it mended.

MARY

Still, it's a dreadful thing to have happened.

JOHN

We'll get it mended, and if Jane is unhappy about it she can have Alice's frame. Alice is too young to notice it.

MARY

She isn't, John. She'd notice it quick.

JOHN

Well, George, then.

MARY [*looking at photo thoughtfully*]

Well, perhaps George might give up his frame.

JOHN

Yes, tell Liza to change it. Why not make her do it now?

MARY

Not to-day, John. Not on a Sunday. She shall do it to-morrow by the time you get back from the office.

IF

JOHN

All right. It might have been worse.

MARY

It's bad enough. I wish it hadn't happened.

JOHN

It might have been worse. It might have been Aunt Martha.

MARY

I'd sooner it had been her than poor little Jane.

JOHN

If it had been Aunt Martha's photograph she'd have walked in next day and seen it for certain; I know Aunt Martha. Then there'd have been trouble.

MARY

But, John, how could she have known?

JOHN

I don't know, but she would have; it's a kind of devilish sense she has.

MARY

John!

JOHN

What's the matter?

IF

MARY

John! What a dreadful word you used. And on a Sunday too! Really!

JOHN

O, I'm sorry. It slipped out somehow. I'm very sorry.

[*Enter* LIZA.]

LIZA

There's a gentleman to see you, sir, which isn't, properly speaking, a gentleman at all. Not what I should call one, that is, like.

MARY

Not a gentleman! Good gracious, Liza! Whatever do you mean?

LIZA

He's black.

MARY

Black?

JOHN [*reassuring*]

O . . . yes, that would be Ali. A queer old customer, Mary; perfectly harmless. Our firm gets hundreds of carpets through him; and then one day . . .

MARY

But what is he doing here, John?

14

IF

JOHN

Well, one day he turned up in London;
broke, he said; and wanted the firm to give
him a little cash. Well, old Briggs was for
giving him ten shillings. But I said "here's
a man that's helped us in making thousands
of pounds. Let's give him fifty."

MARY

Fifty pounds!

JOHN

Yes, it seems a lot; but it seemed only fair.
Ten shillings would have been an insult to
the old fellow, and he'd have taken it as such.
You don't know what he'd have done.

MARY

Well, he doesn't want more?

JOHN

No, I expect he's come to thank me. He
seemed pretty keen on getting some cash.
Badly broke, you see. Don't know what he was
doing in London. Never can tell with these
fellows. East is East, and there's an end of it.

MARY

How did he trace you here?

JOHN

O, got the address at the office. Briggs
and Cater won't let theirs be known. Not
got such a smart little house, I expect.

IF

MARY

I don't like letting people in that you don't know where they come from.

JOHN

O, he comes from the East.

MARY

Yes, I—I know. But the East doesn't seem quite to count, somehow, as the proper sort of place to come from, does it, dear?

JOHN

No.

MARY

It's not like Sydenham or Bromley, some place you can put your finger on.

JOHN

Perhaps just for once, I don't think there's any harm in him.

MARY

Well, just for once. But we can't make a practice of it. And you don't want to be thinking of business on a Sunday, your only day off.

JOHN

O, it isn't business, you know. He only wants to say thank you.

16

IF

MARY

I hope he won't say it in some queer Eastern way. You don't know what these people . . .

JOHN

O, no. Show him up, Liza.

LIZA

As you like, mum.

[*Exit.*]

MARY

And you gave him fifty pounds?

JOHN

Well, old Briggs agreed to it. So I suppose that's what he got. Cater paid him.

MARY

It seems a lot of money. But I think, as the man is actually coming up the stairs, I'm glad he's got something to be grateful for.

[*Enter* ALI, *shown in by* LIZA.]

ALI

Protector of the Just.

JOHN

O, er—yes. Good evening.

IF

ALI

My soul was parched and you bathed it in rivers of gold.

JOHN

O, ah, yes.

ALI

Wherefore the name Briggs, Cater, and Beal shall be magnified and called blessed.

JOHN

Ha, yes. Very good of you.

ALI [*advancing, handing trinket*]

Protector of the Just, my offering.

JOHN

Your offering?

ALI

Hush. It is beyond price. I am not bidden to sell it. I was in my extremity, but I was not bidden to sell it. It is a token of gratitude, a gift, as it came to me.

JOHN

As it came to you?

ALI

Yes, it was given me.

18

IF

JOHN

I see. Then you had given somebody what you call rivers of gold?

ALI

Not gold; it was in Sahara.

JOHN

O, and what do you give in the Sahara instead of gold?

ALI

Water.

JOHN

I see. You got it for a glass of water, like.

ALI

Even so.

JOHN

And—and what happened?

MARY

I wouldn't take his only crystal, dear. It's a nice little thing, but [*to* ALI], but you think a lot of it, don't you?

ALI

Even so.

JOHN

But look here, what does it do?

19

IF

ALI

Much.

JOHN

Well, what?

ALI

He that taketh this crystal, so, in his hand, at night, and wishes, saying "At a certain hour let it be"; the hour comes and he will go back eight, ten, even twelve years if he will, into the past, and do a thing again, or act otherwise than he did. The day passes; the ten years are accomplished once again; he is here once more; but he is what he might have become had he done that one thing otherwise.

MARY

John!

JOHN

I—I don't understand.

ALI

To-night you wish. All to-morrow you live the last ten years; a new way, master, a new way, how you please. To-morrow night you are here, what those years have made you.

JOHN

By Jove!

IF

MARY

Have nothing to do with it, John.

JOHN

All right, Mary, I'm not going to. But, do you mean one could go back ten years?

ALI

Even so.

JOHN

Well, it seems odd, but I'll take your word for it. But look here, you can't live ten years in a day, you know.

ALI

My master has power over time.

MARY

John, don't have anything to do with him.

JOHN

All right, Mary. But who is your master?

ALI

He is carved of one piece of jade, a god in the greenest mountains. The years are his dreams. This crystal is his treasure. Guard it safely, for his power is in this more than in all the peaks of his native hills. See what I give you, master.

IF

JOHN

Well, really, it's very good of you.

MARY

Good night, Mr. Ali. We are very much
obliged for your kind offer, which we are so
sorry we can't avail ourselves of.

JOHN

One moment, Mary. Do you mean that
I can go back ten years, and live till—till now
again, and only be away a day?

ALI

Start early, and you will be here before
midnight.

JOHN

Would eight o'clock do!

ALI

You could be back by eleven that evening.

JOHN

I don't quite see how ten years could go
in a single day.

ALI

They will go as dreams go.

JOHN

Even so, it seems rather unusual, doesn't
it?

IF

ALI

Time is the slave of my master.

MARY

John!

JOHN

All right, Mary. [*In a lower voice.*] I'm
only trying to see what he'll say.

MARY

All right, John, only . . .

ALI

Is there no step that you would wish un-
trodden, nor stride that you would make
where once you faltered?

JOHN

I say, why don't you use it yourself?

ALI

I? I am afraid of the past. But you
Engleesh, and the great firm of Briggs, Cater,
and Beal; you are afraid of nothing.

JOHN

Ha, ha. Well—I wouldn't go quite as far
as that, but—well, give me the crystal.

MARY

Don't take it, John! Don't take it.

IF

JOHN
Why, Mary? It won't hurt me.

MARY
If it can do all that—if it can do all that . . .

JOHN
Well?

MARY
Why, you might never have met me.

JOHN
Never have met you? I never thought of that.

MARY
Leave the past alone, John.

JOHN
All right, Mary. I needn't use it. But I want to hear about it, it's so odd, it's so what-you-might-call queer; I don't think I ever—— [*To* ALI.] You mean if I work hard for ten years, which will only be all to-morrow, I may be Governor of the Bank of England to-morrow night.

ALI
Even so.

MARY
O, don't do it, John.

24

IF

JOHN

But you said—I'll be back here before midnight to-morrow.

ALI

It is so.

JOHN

But the Governor of the Bank of England would live in the City, and he'd have a much bigger house anyway. He wouldn't live in Lewisham.

ALI

The crystal will bring you to this house when the hour is accomplished, even to-morrow night. If you be the great banker, you will perhaps come to chastise one of your slaves who will dwell in this house. If you be head of Briggs and Cater you will come to give an edict to one of your firm. Perchance this street will be yours and you will come to show your power unto it. *But you will come.*

JOHN

And if the house is not mine?

MARY

John! John! Don't.

ALI

Still you will come.

25

IF

JOHN

Shall I remember?

ALI

No.

JOHN

If I want to do anything different to what I did, how shall I remember when I get back there?

MARY

Don't. Don't do anything different, John.

JOHN

All right.

ALI

Choose just before the hour of the step you desire to change. Memory lingers a little at first, and fades away slowly.

JOHN

Five minutes?

ALI

Even ten.

JOHN

Then I can change one thing. After that I forget.

ALI

Even so. One thing. And the rest follows.

26

IF

JOHN

Well, it's very good of you to make me this
nice present, I'm sure.

ALI

Sell it not. Give it, as I gave it, if the heart
impels. So shall it come back one day to the
hills that are brighter than grass, made richer
by the gratitude of many men. And my
master shall smile thereat and the vale shall
be glad.

JOHN

It's very good of you, I'm sure.

MARY

I don't like it, John. I don't like tampering
with what's gone.

ALI

My master's power is in your hands.
Farewell.
[*Exit.*]

JOHN

I say, he's gone.

MARY

O, he's a dreadful man.

JOHN

I never really meant to take it.

IF

MARY

O, John, I wish you hadn't

JOHN

Why? I'm not going to use it.

MARY

Not going to use it, John?

JOHN

No, no. Not if you don't want me to.

MARY

O, I'm so glad.

JOHN

And besides, I don't want things different. I've got fond of this little house. And Briggs is a good old sort, you know. Cater's a bit of an ass, but there's no harm in him. In fact, I'm contented, Mary. I wouldn't even change Aunt Martha now.

[*Points at frowning framed photograph centrally hung.*]

You remember when she first came and you said "Where shall we hang her?" I said the cellar. You said we couldn't. So she had to go there. But I wouldn't change her now. I suppose there are old watch-dogs like her in every family. I wouldn't change anything.

MARY

O, John, wouldn't you really?

28

IF

JOHN

No, I'm contented. Grim old soul, I wouldn't even change Aunt Martha.

MARY

I'm glad of that, John. I was frightened. I couldn't bear to tamper with the past. You don't know what it is, it's what's gone. But if it really isn't gone at all, if it can be dug up like that, why you don't know what mightn't happen! I don't mind the future, but if the past can come back like that. . . . O, don't, don't, John. Don't think of it. It isn't canny. There's the children, John.

JOHN

Yes, yes, that's all right. It's only a little ornament. I won't use it. And I tell you I'm content. [*Happily*] It's no use to me.

MARY

I'm so glad you're content, John. Are you really? Is there nothing that you'd have had different? I sometimes thought you'd rather that Jane had been a boy.

JOHN

Not a bit of it. Well, I may have at the time, but Arthur's good enough for me.

MARY

I'm so glad. And there's nothing you ever regret at all?

IF

JOHN

Nothing. And you? Is there nothing you regret, Mary?

MARY

Me? Oh, no. I still think that sofa would have been better green, but you would have it red.

JOHN

Yes, so I would. No, there's nothing I regret.

MARY

I don't suppose there's many men can say that.

JOHN

No, I don't suppose they can. ·They're not all married to you. I don't suppose many of them can.

[MARY *smiles*.]

MARY

I should think that very few could say that they regretted nothing . . . very few in the whole world.

JOHN

Well, I won't say nothing.

MARY

What is it you regret, John?

30

IF

JOHN

Well, there is one thing.

MARY

And what is that?

JOHN

One thing has rankled a bit.

MARY

Yes, John?

JOHN

O, it's nothing, it's nothing worth mentioning. But it rankled for years.

MARY

What was it, John?

JOHN

O, it seems silly to mention it. It was nothing.

MARY

But what?

JOHN

O, well, if you want to know, it was once when I missed a train. I don't mind missing a train, but it was the way the porter pushed me out of the way. He pushed me by the face. I couldn't hit back, because, well, you know what lawyers make of it; I might have been ruined. So it just rankled. It was years ago before we married.

MARY

Pushed you by the face. Good gracious!

JOHN

Yes, I'd like to have caught that train in spite of him. I sometimes think of it still. Silly of me, isn't it?

MARY

What a brute of a man.

JOHN

O, I suppose he was doing his silly duty. But it rankled.

MARY

He'd no right to do any such thing! He'd no right to touch you!

JOHN

O, well, never mind.

MARY

I should like to have been there. . . . I'd have . . .

JOHN

O, well, it can't be helped now; but I'd like to have caught it in sp . . .

[*An idea seizes him.*]

IF

MARY

What is it?

JOHN

Can't be helped, I said. *It's the very thing that can be helped.*

MARY

Can be helped, John? Whatever do you mean?

JOHN

I mean he'd no right to stop me catching that train. I've got the crystal, and I'll catch it yet!

MARY

O, John, that's what you said you wouldn't do.

JOHN

No. I said I'd do nothing to alter the past. And I won't. I'm too content, Mary. But this can't alter it. This is nothing.

MARY

What were you going to catch the train for, John?

JOHN

For London. I wasn't at the office then. It was a business appointment. There was a

man who had promised to get me a job, and
I was going up to . . .

MARY

John, it may alter your whole life!

JOHN

Now do listen, Mary, do listen. He never
turned up. I got a letter from him apologis-
ing to me before I posted mine to him. It
turned out he never meant to help me, mere
meaningless affabilities. He never came to
London that day at all. I should have taken
the next train back. That can't affect the
future.

MARY

N-no, John. Still, I don't like it.

JOHN

What difference could it make?

MARY

N-n-no.

JOHN

Think how we met. We met at Archie's
wedding. I take it one has to go to one's
brother's wedding. It would take a pretty
big change to alter that. And you were her
bridesmaid. We were bound to meet. And
having once met, well, there you are. If we'd
met by chance, in a train, or anything like

34

that, well, then I admit some little change might alter it. But when we met at Archie's wedding and you were her bridesmaid, why, Mary, it's a cert. Besides, I believe in predestination. It was our fate; we couldn't have missed it.

MARY

No, I suppose not; still . . .

JOHN

Well, what?

MARY

I don't like it.

JOHN

O, Mary, I have so longed to catch that infernal train. Just think of it, annoyed on and off for ten years by the eight-fifteen.

MARY

I'd rather you didn't, John.

JOHN

But why?

MARY

O, John, suppose there's a railway accident? You might be killed, and we should never meet.

JOHN

There wasn't.

35

IF

MARY

There wasn't, John? What do you mean?

JOHN

There wasn't an accident to the eight-fifteen. It got safely to London just ten years ago.

MARY

Why, nor there was.

JOHN

You see how groundless your fears are.
I shall catch that train, and all the rest will
happen the same as before. Just think,
Mary, all those old days again. I wish I
could take you with me. But you soon will
be. But just think of the old days coming
back again. Hampton Court again and Kew,
and Richmond Park again with all the May.
And that bun you bought, and the corked
ginger-beer, and those birds singing and the
'bus past Isleworth. O, Mary, you wouldn't
grudge me that?

MARY

Well, well then all right, John.

JOHN

And you will remember there wasn't an
accident, won't you?

MARY [*resignedly, sadly*]

O, yes, John. And you won't try to get
rich or do anything silly, will you?

36

IF

JOHN

No, Mary. I only want to catch that train. I'm content with the rest. The same things must happen, and they must lead me the same way, to you, Mary. Good night, now, dear.

MARY

Good night?

JOHN

I shall stay here on the sofa holding the crystal and thinking. Then I'll have a biscuit and start at seven.

MARY

Thinking, John? What about?

JOHN

Getting it clear in my mind what I want to do. That one thing and the rest the same. There must be no mistakes.

MARY [*sadly*]

Good night, John.

JOHN

Have supper ready at eleven.

MARY

Very well, John.

[*Exit.*]

37

IF

JOHN [*on the sofa, after a moment or two*]
I'll catch that infernal train in spite of him.

[*He takes the crystal and closes it up in the palm of his left hand.*]

I wish to go back ten years, two weeks and a day, at, at—8.10 a.m. to-morrow; 8.10 a.m. to-morrow, 8.10.

[*Re-enter* MARY *in doorway.*]

MARY

John! John! You are sure he *did* get his fifty pounds?

JOHN

Yes. Didn't he come to thank me for the money?

MARY

You are sure it wasn't ten shillings?

JOHN

Well, Cater paid him, I didn't.

MARY

Are you sure that Cater didn't give him ten shillings?

JOHN

It's the sort of silly thing Cater *would* have done!

IF

MARY

O, John!

JOHN

Hmm.

Curtain

SCENE 3

Scene: As in Act I, Scene 1.
Time.   Ten years ago.

BERT

'Ow goes it, Bill?

BILL

Goes it?   'Ow d'yer think it goes?

BERT

I don't know, Bill.   'Ow is it?

BILL

Bloody.

BERT

Why, what's wrong?

BILL

Wrong?   Nothing ain't wrong.

BERT

What's up, then?

39

IF

BILL

Nothing ain't right.

BERT

Why, wot's the worry?

BILL

Wot's the worry? They don't give you better wages nor a dog, and then they thinks they can talk at yer and talk at yer, and say wot they likes, like.

BERT

Why? You been on the carpet, Bill?

BILL

Ain't I! Proper.

BERT

Why? Wot about, Bill?

BILL

Wot about? I'll tell yer. Just coz I let a lidy get into a train. That's wot about. Said I ought to 'av stopped 'er. Thought the train was moving. Thought it was dangerous. Thought I tried to murder 'er, I suppose.

BERT

Wot? The other day?

BILL

Yes.

IF

BERT
Tuesday?

BILL
Yes.

BERT
Why? The one that dropped her bag?

BILL
Yes. Drops 'er bag. Writes to the company. They writes back she shouldn't 'av got in. She writes back she should. Then they gets on to me. Any more of it and I'll . . .

BERT
I wouldn't, Bill; don't you.

BILL
I will.

BERT
Don't you, Bill. You've got your family to consider.

BILL
Well, anyway, I won't let any more of them passengers go jumping into trains any more, not when they're moving, I won't. When the train gets in, doors shut. That's the rule, and they'll have to abide by it.

[*Enter* JOHN BEAL.]

IF

BILL [*touching his hat*]

Good morning, sir.

[JOHN *does not answer, but walks to the door between them.*]

Carry your bag, sir?

JOHN

Go to hell!

[*Exit through door.*]

BILL

Ullo.

BERT

Somebody's been getting at 'im.

BILL

Well, I never did. Why, I knows the young feller.

BERT

Pleasant spoken, ain't 'e, as a rule?

BILL

Never knew 'im like this.

BERT

You ain't bin sayin' nothing to 'im, 'ave yer?

BILL

Never in my life.

IF

BERT

Well, I never.

BILL

'Ad some trouble o' some kind.

BERT

Must 'ave.

[*Train is heard.*]

BILL

Ah, 'ere she is. Well, as I was saying . . .

Curtain

SCENE 4

In a second-class railway carriage.

Time: Same morning as Scene 1, Act I.
Noise, and a scene drawn past the
windows. The scene, showing a momen-
tary glimpse of fair English hills, is al-
most entirely placards, "GIVE HER
BOVRIL," "GIVE HER OXO," alter-
nately, for ever.

Occupants, JOHN BEAL, a girl, a man.

All sit in stoical silence like the two
images near Luxor. The man has the
window seat, and therefore the right of
control over the window.

43

IF

MIRALDA CLEMENT

Would you mind having the window open?

THE MAN IN THE CORNER [*shrugging his shoulders in a shivery way*]

Er—certainly. [*Meaning he does not mind. He opens the window.*]

MIRALDA CLEMENT

Thank you so much.

MAN IN THE CORNER

Not at all. [*He does not mean to contradict her. Stoical silence again.*]

MIRALDA CLEMENT

Would you mind having it shut now? I think it is rather cold.

MAN IN THE CORNER

Certainly.
[*He shuts it. Silence again.*]

MIRALDA CLEMENT

I think I'd like the window open again now for a bit. It is rather stuffy, isn't it?

MAN IN THE CORNER

Well, I think it's very cold.

44

IF

MIRALDA CLEMENT

O, do you?   But would you mind opening
it for me?

MAN IN THE CORNER

I'd much rather it was shut, if you don't
mind.

> [*She sighs, moves her hands slightly, and
> her pretty face expresses the resignation of
> the Christian martyr in the presence of
> lions.   This for the benefit of John.*]

JOHN

Allow me, madam.

> [*He leans across the window's rightful
> owner, a bigger man than he, and opens his
> window.*
>
> MAN IN THE CORNER *shrugs his shoul-
> ders and, quite sensibly, turns to his paper.*]

MIRALDA

O, thank you *so* much.

JOHN

Don't mention it.

> [*Silence again.*]

VOICES OF PORTERS [*off*]

Fan Kar, Fan Kar.

> [MAN IN THE CORNER *gets out.*]

45

IF

MIRALDA

Could you tell me where this is?

JOHN

Yes. Elephant and Castle.

MIRALDA

Thank you so much. It *was* kind of you to
protect me from that horrid man. He wanted
to suffocate me.

JOHN

O, very glad to assist you, I'm sure. Very
glad.

MIRALDA

I should have been afraid to have done it in
spite of him. It was splendid of you.

JOHN

O, that was nothing.

MIRALDA

O, it was, really.

JOHN

Only too glad to help you in any little way.

MIRALDA

It *was* so kind of you.

46

IF

JOHN

O, not at all.

[*Silence for a bit.*]

MIRALDA

I've nobody to help me.

JOHN

Er, er, haven't you really?

MIRALDA

No, nobody.

JOHN

I'd be very glad to help you in any little way.

MIRALDA

I wonder if you could advise me.

JOHN

I—I'd do my best.

MIRALDA

You see, I have nobody to advise me.

JOHN

No, of course not.

MIRALDA

I live with my aunt, and she doesn't understand. I've no father or mother.

47

IF

JOHN

O, er, er, really?

MIRALDA

No. And an uncle died and he left me a
hundred thousand pounds.

JOHN

Really?

MIRALDA

Yes. He didn't like me. I think he did it
out of contrariness as much as anything.
He was always like that to me.

JOHN

Was he? Was he really?

MIRALDA

Yes. It was invested at twenty-five per
cent. He never liked me. Thought I was
too—I don't know what.

JOHN

No.

MIRALDA

That was five years ago, and I've never got
a penny of it.

JOHN

Really. But, but that's not right.

IF

MIRALDA [*sadly*]

No.

JOHN

Where's it invested?

MIRALDA

In Al Shaldomir.

JOHN

Where's that?

MIRALDA

I don't quite know. I never was good at
geography. I never quite knew where Persia
ends.

JOHN

And what kind of an investment was it?

MIRALDA

There's a pass in some mountains that they
can get camels over, and a huge toll is levied
on everything that goes by; that is the custom
of the tribe that lives there, and I believe
the toll is regularly collected.

JOHN

And who gets it?

MIRALDA

The chief of the tribe. He is called Ben
Hussein. But my uncle lent him all this

4   49

money, and the toll on the camels was what
they call the security. They always carry
gold and turquoise, you know.

JOHN

Do they?

MIRALDA

Yes, they get it from the rivers.

JOHN

I see.

MIRALDA

It does seem a shame his not paying,
doesn't it?

JOHN

A shame? I should think it is. An awful
shame. Why, it's a crying shame. He ought
to go to prison.

MIRALDA

Yes, he ought. But you see it's so hard
to find him. It isn't as if it was this side of
Persia. It's being on the other side that is
such a pity. If only it was in a country like,
like . . .

JOHN

I'd soon find him. I'd . . . Why, a man
like that deserves anything.

50

IF

MIRALDA

It is good of you to say that.

JOHN

Why, I'd . . . And you say you never got a penny?

MIRALDA

No.

JOHN

Well, that is a shame. I call that a down-right shame..

MIRALDA

Now, what ought I to do?

JOHN

Do? Well, now, you know in business there's nothing like being on the spot. When you're on the spot you can—but then, of course, it's so far.

MIRALDA

It is, isn't it?

JOHN

Still, I think you should go if you could. If only I could offer to help you in any way, I would gladly, but of course . . .

MIRALDA

What would you do?

IF

JOHN

I'd go and find that Hussein fellow; and then . . .

MIRALDA

Yes?

JOHN

Why, I'd tell him a bit about the law, and make him see that you didn't keep all that money that belonged to someone else.

MIRALDA

Would you really?

JOHN ·

Nothing would please me better.

MIRALDA

Would you really? Would you go all that way?

JOHN

It's just the sort of thing that I should like, apart from the crying shame. The man ought to be . . .

MIRALDA

We're getting into Holborn. Would you come and lunch somewhere with me and talk it over?

JOHN

Gladly. I'd be glad to help. I've got to
see a man on business first. I've come up to
see him. And then after that, after that,
there was something I wanted to do after that.
I can't think what it was. But something I
wanted to do after that. O, heavens, what
was it?
[*Pause.*]

MIRALDA

Can't you think?

JOHN

No. O, well, it can't have been so very
important. And yet . . . Well, where shall
we lunch?

MIRALDA

Gratzenheim's.

JOHN

Right. What time?

MIRALDA

One-thirty. Would that suit?

JOHN

Perfectly. I'd like to get a man like Hussein in prison. I'd like . . . O, I beg your
pardon.

> [*He hurries to open the door. Exit*
> MIRALDA.]

IF

Now what was it I wanted to do afterwards?

[*Throws hand to forehead.*]

O, never mind.

Curtain

ACT II

JOHN'S *tent in Al Shaldomir. There are two heaps of idols, left and right, lying upon the ground inside the tent.* DAOUD *carries another idol in his arms.* JOHN *looks at its face.*
Six months have elapsed since the scene in the second-class railway carriage.

JOHN BEAL

This god is holy.
[*He points to the left heap.* DAOUD *carries it there and lays it on the heap.*]

DAOUD

Yes, great master.

JOHN BEAL

You are in no wise to call me great master. Have not I said so? I am not your master. I am helping you people. I know better than you what you ought to do, because I am English. But that's all. I'm not your master. See?

55

IF

DAOUD

Yes, great master.

JOHN BEAL

O, go and get some more idols. Hurry.

DAOUD

Great master, I go.
    [*Exit.*]

JOHN BEAL

I can't make these people out.

DAOUD [*returning*]

I have three gods.

JOHN BEAL [*looking at their faces, pointing to
        the two smaller idols first*]

These two are holy. This one is unholy.

DAOUD

Yes, great master.

JOHN BEAL

Put them on the heap.
    [DAOUD *does so, two left, one right.*]
Get some more.
    [DAOUD *salaams.   Exit.*]

[*Looking at right heap.*] What a—what a filthy people.

[*Enter* DAOUD *with two idols.*]

JOHN BEAL [*after scrutiny*]

This god is holy, this is unholy.

[*Enter* ARCHIE BEAL, *wearing a "Bow-ler" hat.*]

Why, Archie, this is splendid of you! You've come! Why, that's splendid! All that way!

ARCHIE BEAL

Yes, I've come. Whatever are you doing?

JOHN BEAL

Archie, it's grand of you to come! I never ought to have asked it of you, only . . .

ARCHIE BEAL

O, that's all right. But what in the world are you doing?

JOHN BEAL

Archie, it's splendid of you.

ARCHIE BEAL

O, cut it. That's all right. But what's all this?

JOHN BEAL

O, this. Well, well they're the very oddest people here. It's a long story. But I wanted

57

to tell you first how enormously grateful I am to you for coming.

ARCHIE BEAL

O, that's all right. But I want to know what you're doing with all these genuine antiques.

JOHN BEAL

Well, Archie, the fact of it is they're a real odd lot of people here. I've learnt their language, more or less, but I don't think I quite understand them yet. A lot of them are Mahommedans; they worship Mahommed, you know. He's dead. But a lot of them worship these things, and . . .

ARCHIE BEAL

Well, what have you got 'em all in here for?

JOHN BEAL

Yes, that's just it. I hate interfering with them, but, well, I simply had to. You see there's two sorts of idols here; they offer fruit and rats to some of them; they lay them on their hands or their laps.

ARCHIE BEAL

Why do they offer them rats?

JOHN BEAL

O, I don't know. They don't know either. It's the right thing to do out here, it's been

IF

the right thing for hundreds of years; nobody
exactly knows why. It's like the bows we
have on evening shoes, or anything else.
But it's all right.

ARCHIE BEAL

Well, what are you putting them in heaps
for?

JOHN BEAL

Because there's the other kind, the ones
with wide mouths and rust round them.

ARCHIE BEAL

Rust? Yes, so there is. What do they
do?

JOHN BEAL

They offer blood to them, Archie. They
pour it down their throats. Sometimes they
kill people, sometimes they only bleed them.
It depends how much blood the idol wants.

ARCHIE BEAL

How much blood it wants? Good Lord!
How do they know?

JOHN BEAL

The priests tell them. Sometimes they
fill them up to their necks—they're all hollow,
you know. In spring it's awful.

ARCHIE BEAL

Why are they worse in spring?

59

JOHN BEAL

I don't know. The priests ask for more blood then. Much more. They say it always was so.

ARCHIE BEAL

And you're stopping it?

JOHN BEAL

Yes, I'm stopping these. One must. I'm letting them worship those. Of course, it's idolatry and all that kind of thing, but I don't like interfering short of actual murder.

ARCHIE BEAL

And they're obeying you?

JOHN BEAL

'M, y-yes. I think so.

ARCHIE BEAL

You must have got a great hold over them.

JOHN BEAL

Well, I don't know about that. It's the pass that counts.

ARCHIE BEAL

The pass?

JOHN BEAL

Yes, that place you came over. It's the only way anyone can get here.

ARCHIE BEAL

Yes, I suppose it is. But how does the pass affect these idols?

JOHN BEAL

It affects everything here. If that pass were closed no living man would ever enter or leave, or even hear of, this country. It's absolutely cut off except for that one pass. Why, Archie, it isn't even on the map.

ARCHIE BEAL

Yes, I know.

JOHN BEAL

Well, whoever owns that pass is everybody. No one else counts.

ARCHIE BEAL

And who does own it?

JOHN BEAL

Well, it's actually owned by a fellow called Hussein, but Miss Clement's uncle, a man called Hinnard, a kind of lonely explorer, seems to have come this way; and I think he understood what this pass is worth. Anyhow, he lent Hussein a big sum of money and got an acknowledgment from Hussein. Old Hinnard must have been a wonderfully shrewd man. For that acknowledgment is no more legal than an I.O.U., and Hussein is simply a brigand.

IF

ARCHIE BEAL

Not very good security.

JOHN BEAL

Well, you're wrong there. Hussein himself
respects that piece of parchment he signed.
There's the name of some god or other written
on it that Hussein is frightened of. Now you
see how things are. That pass is as holy as
all the gods that there are in Al Shaldomir.
Hussein possesses it. But he owes an enormous sum to Miss Miralda Clement, and I am
here as her agent; and you've come to help
me like a great sportsman.

ARCHIE BEAL

O, never mind that. Well, it all seems
pretty simple.

JOHN BEAL

Well, I don't know, Archie. Hussein
admits the debt, but . . .

ARCHIE BEAL

But what?

JOHN BEAL

I don't know what he'll do.

ARCHIE BEAL

Wants watching, does he?

62

JOHN BEAL

Yes. And meanwhile I feel sort of responsible for all these silly people. Somebody's got to look after them. Daoud!

DAOUD [*off*]

Great master.

JOHN BEAL

Bring in some more gods.

DAOUD

Yes, great master.

JOHN BEAL

I can't get them to stop calling me absurd titles. They're so infernally Oriental.

[*Enter* DAOUD.]

ARCHIE BEAL

He's got two big ones this time.

JOHN BEAL [*to* ARCHIE]
You see, there is rust about their mouths.
[*To* DAOUD]: They are both unholy.
[*He points to R. heap, and* DAOUD
puts them there. To DAOUD.]
Bring in some more.

DAOUD

Great master, there are no more gods in Al Shaldomir.

IF

JOHN BEAL
It is well.

DAOUD
What orders, great master.

JOHN BEAL
Listen. At night you shall come and take
these gods away. These shall be worshipped
again in their own place, these you shall cast
into the great river and tell no man where you
cast them.

DAOUD
Yes, great master.

JOHN BEAL
You will do this, Daoud?

DAOUD
Even so, great master.

JOHN BEAL
I am sorry to make you do it. You are
sad that you have to do it. Yet it must be
done.

DAOUD
Yes, I am sad, great master.

JOHN BEAL
But why are you sad, Daoud?

64

IF

DAOUD

Great master, in times you do not know
these gods were holy. In times you have not
guessed. In old centuries, master, perhaps
before the pass. Men have prayed to them,
sorrowed before them, given offerings to
them. The light of old hearths has shone on
them, flames from old battles. The shadow
of the mountains has fallen on them, so
many times, master, so many times. Dawn
and sunset have shone on them, master, like
firelight flickering; dawn and sunset, dawn
and sunset, flicker, flicker, flicker for century
after century. They have sat there watching
the dawns like old men by the fire. They are
so old, master, so old. And some day dawn
and sunset will die away and shine on the
world no more, and they would have still
sat on in the cold. And now they go. . . .
They are our history, master, they are our old
times. Though they be bad times they are
our times, master; and now they go. I am
sad, master, when the old gods go.

JOHN BEAL

But they are bad gods, Daoud.

DAOUD

I am sad when the bad gods go.

JOHN BEAL

They must go, Daoud. See, there is no
one watching. Take them now.

IF

DAOUD

Even so, great master.

[*He takes up the largest of the gods with rust.*]

Come, Aho-oomlah, thou shalt not drink Nideesh.

JOHN BEAL

Was Nideesh to have been sacrificed?

DAOUD

He was to have been drunk by Aho-oomlah.

JOHN BEAL

Nideesh. Who is he?

DAOUD

He is my son.

[*Exit with Aho-oomlah.*

JOHN BEAL *almost gasps.*]

ARCHIE BEAL [*who has been looking round the tent*]

What has he been saying?

JOHN BEAL

They're—they're a strange people. I can't make them out.

ARCHIE BEAL

Is that the heap that oughtn't to be worshipped?

66

IF

JOHN BEAL

Yes.

ARCHIE BEAL

Well, do you know, I'm going to chuck this hat there. It doesn't seem to me somehow to be any more right here than those idols would be at home. Odd isn't it? Here goes.

[He throws hat on right heap of idols. JOHN BEAL *does not smile.]*

Why, what's the matter?

JOHN BEAL

I don't like to see a decent Christian hat among these filthy idols. They've all got rust on their mouths. I don't like to see it, Archie; it's sort of like what they call an omen. I don't like it.

ARCHIE BEAL

Do they keep malaria here?

JOHN BEAL

I don't think so. Why?

ARCHIE BEAL

Then what's the matter, Johnny? Your nerves are bad.

JOHN BEAL

You don't know these people, and I've brought you out here. I feel kind of responsible. If Hussein's lot turn nasty you don't know what he'd do, with all those idols and all.

ARCHIE BEAL

He'll give 'em a drink, you mean.

JOHN BEAL

Don't, Archie. There's no saying. And I feel responsible for you.

ARCHIE BEAL

Well, they can have my hat. It looks silly, somehow. I don't know why. What are we going to do?

JOHN BEAL

Well, now that you've come we can go ahead.

ARCHIE BEAL

Righto. What at?

JOHN BEAL

We've got to see Hussein's accounts, and get everything clear in black and white, and see just what he owes to Miss Miralda Clement.

ARCHIE BEAL

But they don't keep accounts here.

JOHN BEAL

How do you know?

IF

ARCHIE BEAL

Why, of course they don't. One can see that.

JOHN BEAL

But they must.

ARCHIE BEAL

Well, you haven't changed a bit for your six months here.

JOHN BEAL

Haven't changed?

ARCHIE BEAL

No. Just quietly thinking of business. You'll be a great business man, Johnny.

JOHN BEAL

But we must do business; that's what I came here for.

ARCHIE BEAL

You'll never make these people do it.

JOHN BEAL

Well, what do you suggest?

ARCHIE BEAL

Let's have a look at old Hussein.

IF

JOHN BEAL

Yes, that's what I have been waiting for.
Daoud!

DAOUD [*off*]

Master. [*Enters.*]

JOHN BEAL

Go to the palace of the Lord of the Pass
and beat on the outer door. Say that I desire to see him. Pray him to come to my
tent.

[DAOUD *bows and Exit.*]

[*To* ARCHIE.] I've sent him to the palace
to ask Hussein to come.

ARCHIE BEAL

Lives in a palace, does he?

JOHN BEAL

Yes, it's a palace, it's a wonderful place.
It's bigger than the Mansion House, much.

ARCHIE BEAL

And you're going to teach him to keep
accounts.

JOHN BEAL

Well, I must. I hate doing it. It seems
almost like being rude to the Lord Mayor.
But there's two things I can't stand—cheat-

ing in business is one and murder's another.
I've got to interfere. You see, if one happens
to know the right from wrong as we do, we've
simply got to tell people who don't. But
it isn't pleasant. I almost wish I'd never
come.

ARCHIE BEAL

Why, it's the greatest sport in the world.
It's splendid.

JOHN BEAL

I don't see it that way. To me those idols
are just horrid murder. And this man owes
money to this girl with no one to look after
her, and he's got to pay. But I hate being
rude to a man in a place like the Mansion
House, even if he is black. Why, good Lord,
who am I? It seems such cheek.

ARCHIE BEAL

I say, Johnny, tell me about the lady. Is
she pretty?

JOHN BEAL

What, Miss Miralda? Yes.

ARCHIE BEAL

But what I mean is—what's she like?

JOHN BEAL

Oh, I don't know. It's very hard to say.
She's, she's tall and she's fair and she's got
blue eyes.

IF

ARCHIE BEAL

Yes, but I mean what kind of a person is she? How does she strike you?

JOHN BEAL

Well, she's pretty hard up until she gets this money, and she hasn't got any job that's any good, and no real prospects bar this, and nobody particular by birth, and doesn't know anybody who is, and lives in the least fashionable suburb and can only just afford a second-class fare and . . .

ARCHIE BEAL

Yes, yes, go on.

JOHN BEAL

And yet somehow she sort of seems like a—like a queen.

ARCHIE BEAL

Lord above us! And what kind of a queen?

JOHN BEAL

O, I don't know. Well, look here, Archie, it's only my impression. I don't know her well yet. It's only my impression. I only tell you in absolute confidence. You won't pass it on to anybody, of course.

ARCHIE BEAL

O, no. Go on.

IF

JOHN BEAL

Well, I don't know, only she seemed more like—well, a kind of autocrat, you know, who'd stop at nothing. Well, no, I don't mean that, only . . .

ARCHIE BEAL

So you're not going to marry her?

JOHN BEAL

Marry her! Good Lord, no. Why, you'd never dare ask her. She's not that sort. I tell you she's a sort of queen. And (Good Lord!) she'd *be* a queen if it wasn't for Hussein, or something very like one. We can't go marrying queens. Anyhow, not one like her.

ARCHIE BEAL

Why not one like her?

JOHN BEAL

I tell you—she's a—well, a kind of goddess. You couldn't ask her if she loved you. It would be such, such . . .

ARCHIE BEAL

Such what?

JOHN BEAL

Such infernal cheek.

73

IF

ARCHIE BEAL

I see. Well, I see you aren't in love with her. But it seems to me you'll be seeing a good deal of her some day if we pull this off. And then, my boy-o, you'll be going and getting in love with her.

JOHN BEAL

I tell you I daren't. I'd as soon propose to the Queen of Sheba.

ARCHIE BEAL

Well, Johnny, I'm going to protect you from her all I can.

JOHN BEAL

Protect me from her? Why?

ARCHIE BEAL

Why, because there's lots of other girls, and it seems to me you might be happier with some of them.

JOHN BEAL

But you haven't even seen her.

ARCHIE BEAL

Nor I have. Still, if I'm here to protect you I somehow think I will. And if I'm not
. . .

74

JOHN BEAL

Well, and what then?

ARCHIE BEAL

What nonsense I'm talking. Fate does everything. I can't protect you.

JOHN BEAL

Yes, it's nonsense all right, Archie, but . . .

HUSSEIN [*off*]

I am here.

JOHN BEAL

Be seen.

[HUSSEIN *enters. He is not unlike Bluebeard.*]

JOHN BEAL [*pointing to* ARCHIE]
My brother.

[ARCHIE *shakes hands with* HUSSEIN. HUSSEIN *looks at his hand when it is over in a puzzled way.* JOHN BEAL *and* HUSSEIN *then bow to each other.*]

HUSSEIN

You desired my presence.

JOHN BEAL

I am honoured.

75

IF

HUSSEIN
And I.

JOHN BEAL
The white traveller, whom we call Hinnard, lent you one thousand greater gold pieces, which in our money is one hundred thousand pounds, as you acknowledge. [HUSSEIN *nods his head.*] And every year you were to pay him for this two hundred and fifty of your greater gold pieces—as you acknowledge also.

HUSSEIN
Even so.

JOHN BEAL
And this you have not yet had chance to pay, but owe it still.

HUSSEIN
I do.

JOHN BEAL
And now Hinnard is dead.

HUSSEIN
Peace be with him.

JOHN BEAL
His heiress is Miss Miralda Clement, who instructs me to be her agent. What have you to say?

IF

HUSSEIN

Peace be with Hinnard.

JOHN BEAL

You acknowledge your debt to this lady,
Miss Miralda Clement?

HUSSEIN

I know her not.

JOHN BEAL

You will not pay your debt?

HUSSEIN

I will pay.

JOHN BEAL

If you bring the gold to my tent, my
brother will take it to Miss Clement.

HUSSEIN

I do not pay to Miss Clement.

JOHN BEAL

To whom do you pay?

HUSSEIN

I pay to Hinnard.

JOHN BEAL

Hinnard is dead.

IF

HUSSEIN

I pay to Hinnard.

JOHN BEAL

How will you pay to Hinnard?

HUSSEIN

If he be buried in the sea . . .

JOHN BEAL

He is not buried at sea.

HUSSEIN

If he be buried by any river I go to the god
of rivers.

JOHN BEAL

He is buried on land near no river.

HUSSEIN

Therefore I will go to a bronze god of
earth, very holy, having the soil in his care,
and the things of earth. I will take unto him
the greater pieces of gold due up to the year
when the white traveller died, and will melt
them in fire at his feet by night on the mountains, saying, "O, Lruru-onn (this is his
name) take this by the way of earth to the
grave of Hinnard." And so I shall be free
of my debt before all gods.

JOHN BEAL

But not before me. I am English. And
we are greater than gods.

ARCHIE BEAL

What's that, Johnny?

JOHN BEAL

He won't pay, but I told him we're English
and that they're greater than all his bronze
gods.

ARCHIE BEAL

That's right, Johnny.

[HUSSEIN *looks fiercely at* ARCHIE.
He sees ARCHIE'S *hat lying before a big
idol. He points at the hat and looks in
the face of the idol.*]

HUSSEIN [*to the idol*]

Drink! Drink!

[*He bows. Exit.*]

ARCHIE BEAL

What's that he's saying?

JOHN BEAL [*meditatively*]

O, nothing—nothing.

ARCHIE BEAL

He won't pay, eh?

79

IF

JOHN BEAL

No, not to Miss Miralda.

ARCHIE BEAL

Who to?

JOHN BEAL

To one of his gods.

ARCHIE BEAL

That won't do.

JOHN BEAL

No.

ARCHIE BEAL

What'll we do?

JOHN BEAL

I don't quite know. It isn't as if we were in England.

ARCHIE BEAL

No, it isn't.

JOHN BEAL

If we were in England . . .

ARCHIE BEAL

I know; if we were in England you could call a policeman. I tell you what it is, Johnny.

80

JOHN BEAL

Yes?

ARCHIE BEAL

I tell you what; you want to see more of Miss Clement.

JOHN BEAL

Why?

ARCHIE BEAL

Why, because at the present moment our friend Hussein is a craftier fellow than you, and looks like getting the best of it.

JOHN BEAL

How will seeing more of Miss Miralda help us?

ARCHIE BEAL

Why, because you want to be a bit craftier than Hussein, and I fancy she might make you.

JOHN BEAL

She? How?

ARCHIE BEAL

We're mostly made what we are by some woman or other. We think it's our own cleverness, but we're wrong. As things are you're no match for Hussein, but if you altered . . .

IF

JOHN BEAL

Why, Archie; where did you get all those ideas from?

ARCHIE BEAL

O, I don't know.

JOHN BEAL

You never used to talk like that.

ARCHIE BEAL

O, well.

JOHN BEAL

You haven't been getting in love, Archie, have you?

ARCHIE BEAL

What are we to do about Hussein?

JOHN BEAL

It's funny your mentioning Miss Miralda. I got a letter from her the same day I got yours.

ARCHIE BEAL

What does she say?

JOHN BEAL

I couldn't make it out.

ARCHIE BEAL

What were her words?

IF

JOHN BEAL

She said she was going into it closer. She underlined closer. What could she mean by that? How could she get closer?

ARCHIE BEAL

Well, the same way as I did.

JOHN BEAL

How do you mean? I don't understand.

ARCHIE BEAL

By coming here.

JOHN BEAL

By coming here? But she can't come here.

ARCHIE BEAL

Why not?

JOHN BEAL

Because it's impossible. Absolutely impossible. Why—good Lord—she couldn't come here. Why, she'd want a chaperon and a house and—and—everything. Good Lord, she couldn't come here. It would be—well, it would be impossible—it couldn't be done.

ARCHIE BEAL

O, all right. Then I don't know what she meant.

John Beal

Archie! You don't really think she'd come here? You don't really think it, do you?

Archie Beal

Well, it's the sort of thing that that sort of girl might do, but of course I can't say . . .

John Beal

Good Lord, Archie! That would be awful.

Archie Beal

But why?

John Beal

Why? But what would I do? Where would she go? Where would her chaperon go? The chaperon would be some elderly lady. Why, it would kill her.

Archie Beal

Well, if it did you've never met her, so you needn't go into mourning for an elderly lady that you don't know; not *yet*, anyway.

John Beal

No, of course not. You're laughing at me, Archie. But for the moment I took you seriously. Of course, she won't come. One can go into a thing closely without doing it absolutely literally. But, good Lord, wouldn't it be an awful situation if she did.

IF

ARCHIE BEAL

O, I don't know.

JOHN BEAL

All alone with me here? No, impossible.
And the country isn't civilised.

ARCHIE BEAL

Women aren't civilised.

JOHN BEAL

Women aren't . . . ? Good Lord, Archie,
what an awful remark. What *do* you mean?

ARCHIE BEAL

We're tame, they're wild. We like all the
dull things and the quiet things, they like
all the romantic things and the dangerous
things.

JOHN BEAL

Why, Archie, it's just the other way about.

ARCHIE BEAL

O, yes; we *do* all the romantic things, and
all the dangerous things. But why?

JOHN BEAL

Why? Because we like them, I suppose.
I can't think of any other reason.

IF

ARCHIE BEAL

I hate danger. Don't you?

JOHN BEAL

Er—well, yes, I suppose I do, really.

ARCHIE BEAL

Of course you do. We all do. It's the women that put us up to it. She's putting you up to this. And the more she puts you up to the more likely is Hussein to get it in his fat neck.

JOHN BEAL

But—but you don't mean you'd hurt Hussein? Not—not badly, I mean.

ARCHIE BEAL

We're under her orders, Johnny. See what she says.

JOHN BEAL

You, you don't really think she'll come here?

ARCHIE BEAL

Of course I do, and the best thing too. It's her show; she ought to come.

JOHN BEAL

But, but you don't understand. She's just a young girl. A girl like Miss Miralda

couldn't come out here over the pass and
down these mountains, she'd never stand it,
and as for the chaperon . . .   You've
never met Miss Miralda.

ARCHIE BEAL

No, Johnny. But the girl that was able to
get you to go from Bromley to this place can
look after herself.

JOHN BEAL

I don't see what that's got to do with it.
She was in trouble and I had to help her.

ARCHIE BEAL

Yes, and she'll be in trouble all the way
here from Blackheath, and everyone will have
to help her.

JOHN BEAL

What beats me is how you can have the
very faintest inkling of what she's like without ever having seen her and without my
having spoken of her to you for more than a
minute.

ARCHIE BEAL

Well, Johnny, you're not a romantic bird,
you're not a traveller by nature, barring your
one trip to Eastbourne, and it was I that took
you there. And contrariwise, as they say in
a book you've never read, you're a level-

headed business man and a hardworking respectable stay-at-home. You meet a girl in a train, and the next time I see you you're in a place that isn't marked on the map and telling it what gods it ought to worship and what gods it ought to have agnosticism about. Well, I say *some girl*.

JOHN BEAL

Well, I must say you make the most extraordinary deductions, but it was awfully good of you to come, and I ought to be grateful; and I am, too, I'm awfully grateful; and I ought to let you talk all the rot you like. Go ahead. You shall say what you like and do what you like. It isn't many brothers that would do what you've done.

ARCHIE BEAL

O, that's nothing. I like this country. I'm glad I came. And if I can help you with Hussein, why all the better.

JOHN BEAL

It's an awful country, Archie, but we've got to see this through.

ARCHIE BEAL

Does she know all about Hussein?

JOHN BEAL

Yes, everything. I've written fully.

88

IF

OMAR [*off*]

Al Shaldomir, Al Shaldomir,
The nightingales that guard thy ways . . .

JOHN BEAL [*shouting*]

O, go away, go away. [*To* ARCHIE.] I said
it was an awful country. They sit down outside one's tent and do that kind of thing for
no earthly reason.

ARCHIE BEAL

O, I'd let them sing.

JOHN BEAL

O, you can't have people doing that kind of
thing.

OMAR [*in doorway*]

Master, I go.

JOHN BEAL

But why do you come?

OMAR

I came to sing a joyous song to you, master.

JOHN BEAL

Why did you want to sing me a joyous
song?

OMAR

Because a lady is riding out of the West.
[*Exit.*]

89

IF

JOHN BEAL

A lady out of . . . Good Lord!

ARCHIE BEAL

She's coming, Johnny.

JOHN BEAL

Coming? Good Lord, no, Archie. He said
a lady; there'd be the chaperon too. There'd
be two of them if it was Miss Miralda. But
he said a lady. One lady. It can't be her.
A girl like that alone in Al Shaldomir. Clean
off the map. Oh, no, it isn't possible.

ARCHIE BEAL

I wouldn't worry.

JOHN BEAL

Wouldn't worry? But, good Lord, the
situation's impossible. People would talk.
Don't you see what people would say? And
where could they go? Who would look after
them? Do try and understand how awful
it is. But it isn't. It's impossible. It can't
be them. For heaven's sake run out and see
if it is; and (good Lord!) I haven't brushed
my hair all day, and, and—oh, look at me.

[*He rushes to camp mirror. Exit*
ARCHIE.

JOHN BEAL *tidies up desperately.*

Enter ARCHIE.]

90

IF

ARCHIE BEAL

It's what you call *them.*

JOHN BEAL

What I call *them?* Whatever do you mean?

ARCHIE BEAL

Well, it's her. She's just like what you said.

JOHN BEAL

But it can't be. She doesn't ride. She can never have been able to afford a horse.

ARCHIE BEAL

She's on a camel. She'll be here in a moment. [*He goes to door.*] Hurry up with that hair; she's dismounted.

JOHN BEAL

O, Lord! What's the chaperon like?

ARCHIE BEAL

O, she's attending to that herself.

JOHN BEAL

Attending to it herself? What do you mean?

ARCHIE BEAL

I expect she'll attend to most things.

IF

[*Enter* HAFIZ EL ALCOLAHN *in door-way of tent, pulling back flap a little.*]

JOHN BEAL
Who are you?

HAFIZ
I show the gracious lady to your tent.

[*Enter* MIRALDA CLEMENT, *throwing a smile to* HAFIZ.]

MIRALDA
Hullo, Mr. Beal.

JOHN BEAL
Er—er—how do you do?

[*She looks at* ARCHIE.]

O, this is my brother—Miss Clement.

MIRALDA *and* ARCHIE BEAL
How do you do?

MIRALDA
I like this country.

JOHN BEAL
I'm afraid I hardly expected you.

MIRALDA
Didn't you?

IF

JOHN BEAL

No. You see—er—it's such a long way. And wasn't it very expensive?

MIRALDA

Well, the captain of the ship was very kind to me.

JOHN BEAL

O! But what did you do when you landed?

MIRALDA

O, there were some Arabs coming this way in a caravan. They were really very good to me too.

JOHN BEAL

But the camel?

MIRALDA

O, there were some people the other side of the mountains. Everybody has been very kind about it. And then there was the man who showed me here. He's called Hafiz el Alcolahn. It's a nice name, don't you think?

JOHN BEAL

But, you know, this country, Miss Clement, I'm half afraid it's hardly—isn't it, Archie? Er—how long did you think of staying?

IF

MIRALDA

O, a week or so.

JOHN BEAL

I don't know what you'll think of Al Shaldomir. I'm afraid you'll find it . . .

MIRALDA

Oh, I like it. Just that hollow in the mountains, and the one pass, and no record of it anywhere. I like that. I think it's lovely.

JOHN BEAL

You see, I'm afraid—what I mean is I'm afraid the place isn't even on the map!

MIRALDA

O, that's lovely of it.

JOHN BEAL

All decent places are.

MIRALDA

You mean if a place is on the map we've got to behave accordingly. But if not, why . . .

JOHN BEAL

Hussein won't pay.

MIRALDA

Let's see Hussein.

IF

JOHN BEAL

I'm afraid he's rather, he's rather a savage-looking brigand.

MIRALDA

Never mind.

[ARCHIE *is quietly listening and smiling sometimes.*

Enter DAOUD. *He goes up to the unholy heap and takes away two large idols, one under each arm. Exit.*]

What's that, Mr. Beal?

JOHN BEAL

O, that. I'm afraid it's rather horrible. I told you it was an awful country. They pray to these idols here, and some are all right, though of course it's terribly blasphemous, but *that* heap, well, I'm afraid, well *that* heap is very bad indeed.

MIRALDA

What do they do?

JOHN BEAL

They kill people.

MIRALDA

Do they? How?

IF

JOHN BEAL

I'm afraid they pour their blood down those horrible throats.

MIRALDA

Do they? How do you know?

JOHN BEAL

I've seen them do it, and those mouths are all rusty. But it's all right now. It won't happen any more.

MIRALDA

Won't it? Why not?

JOHN BEAL

Well, I . . .

ARCHIE BEAL

He's stopped them, Miss Clement. They're all going to be thrown into the river.

MIRALDA

Have you?

JOHN BEAL

Well, yes. I had to. So it's all right now. They won't do it any more.

MIRALDA

H'm.

IF

JOHN BEAL

What, what is it? I promise you that's all right. They won't do that any more.

MIRALDA

H'm. I've never known anyone that tried to govern a country or anything of that sort, but . . .

JOHN BEAL

Of course, I'm just doing what I can to put them right. . . . I'd be very glad of your advice. . . . Of course, I'm only here in your name.

MIRALDA

What I mean is that I'd always thought that the one thing you shouldn't do, if you don't mind my saying so.

JOHN BEAL

No, certainly.

MIRALDA

. . . Was to interfere in people's religious beliefs.

JOHN BEAL

But, but I don't think you quite understand. The priests knife these people in the throat, boys and girls, and then acolytes lift them up and the blood runs down. I've seen them.

IF

MIRALDA

I think it's best to leave religion to the priests. They understand that kind of thing.

[JOHN BEAL *opens his mouth in horror and looks at* ARCHIE. ARCHIE *returns the glance; there is very nearly a twinkle in* ARCHIE'S *eyes.*]

MIRALDA

Let's see Hussein.

JOHN BEAL

What do you think, Archie?

ARCHIE BEAL

Poor fellow. We'd better send for him.

MIRALDA

Why do you say "poor fellow"?

ARCHIE BEAL

Oh, because he's so much in debt. It's awful to be in debt. I'd sooner almost anything happened to me than to owe a lot of money.

MIRALDA

Your remark didn't sound very complimentary.

ARCHIE BEAL

O, I only meant that I'd hate to be in debt.

98

And I should hate owing money to you, because . . .

MIRALDA

Why?

ARCHIE BEAL

Because I should so awfully want to pay it.

MIRALDA

I see.

ARCHIE BEAL

That's all I meant.

MIRALDA

Does Hussein awfully want to pay it?

ARCHIE BEAL

Well, no. But he hasn't seen you yet. He will then, of course.

[*Enter* DAOUD. *He goes to the unholy heap.*]

JOHN BEAL

Daoud, for the present these gods must stay. Aho-oomlah's gone, but the rest must stay for the present.

DAOUD

Even so, great master.

JOHN BEAL

Daoud, go once more to the palace of the Lord of the Pass and beat the outer door.

99

IF

Say that the great lady herself would see him.
The great lady, Miss Clement, the white
traveller's heiress.

DAOUD

Yes, master.

JOHN BEAL

Hasten.

[*Exit* DAOUD.]

I have sent him for Hussein.

MIRALDA

I don't know their language.

JOHN BEAL

You will see him, and I'll tell you what he
says.

MIRALDA [*to* ARCHIE]

Have you been here long?

ARCHIE BEAL

No. I think he wrote to me by the same
mail as he wrote to you (if they have mails
here). I came at once.

MIRALDA

So did I; but you weren't on the *Empress
of Switzerland.*

ARCHIE BEAL

No, I came round more by land.

JOHN BEAL

You know, I hardly like bringing Hussein
in here to see you.   He's such a—he's rather
a . . .

MIRALDA

What's the matter with him?

JOHN BEAL

Well, he's rather of the brigand type, and
one doesn't know what he'll do.

MIRALDA

Well, we must see him first and hear what
he has to say before we take any steps.

JOHN BEAL

But what do you propose to do?

MIRALDA

Why, if he pays me everything he owes, or
gives up the security . . .

JOHN BEAL

The security is the pass.

MIRALDA

Yes.   If he gives up that or pays . . .

IF

JOHN BEAL

You know he's practically king of the whole country. It seems rather cheek almost my sending for him like this.

MIRALDA

He must come.

JOHN BEAL

But what are you going to do?

MIRALDA

If he gives up the pass . . .

JOHN BEAL

Why, if he gives up the pass you'd be— you'd be a kind of queen of it all.

MIRALDA

Well, if he does that, all right. . . .

JOHN BEAL

But what if he doesn't?

MIRALDA

Why, if he doesn't pay . . .

HUSSEIN [off]

I am here.

JOHN BEAL

Be seen.

[Enter HUSSEIN.]

102

IF

HUSSEIN

Greeting once more.

JOHN BEAL

Again greeting. . . . The great lady, Miss Clement, is here.

[HUSSEIN *and* MIRALDA *look at each other.*]

You will pay to Miss Clement and not to your god of bronze. On the word of an Englishman, your god of bronze shall not have one gold piece that belongs to the great lady!

HUSSEIN [*looking contemptuous*]

On the word of the Lord of the Pass, I only pay to Hinnard.

[*He stands smiling while* MIRALDA *regards him. Exit.*]

ARCHIE BEAL

Well?

JOHN BEAL

He won't pay.

ARCHIE BEAL

What are we to do now?

JOHN BEAL [*to* MIRALDA]

I'm afraid he's rather an ugly customer to introduce you to like that. I'm sorry he came now.

IF

MIRALDA

O, I like him, I think he looks splendid.

ARCHIE BEAL

Well, what are we to do?

JOHN BEAL

Yes.

ARCHIE BEAL

What do you say, Miss Clement?

JOHN BEAL

Yes, what do you feel we ought to do?

MIRALDA

Well, perhaps I ought to leave all that to you.

ARCHIE BEAL

O, no.

JOHN BEAL

No, it's your money. What do you think we really ought to do?

MIRALDA

Well, of course, I think you ought to kill Hussein.

[JOHN BEAL *and* ARCHIE BEAL *look at each other a little startled.*]

IF

JOHN BEAL

But wouldn't that—wouldn't that be—
murder?

MIRALDA

O, yes, according to the English law.

JOHN BEAL

I see; you mean—you mean we're not—but
we are English.

MIRALDA

I mean it wouldn't be murder—by your
law, unless you made it so.

JOHN BEAL

By *my* law?

MIRALDA

Yes, if you can interfere with their religion
like this, and none of them say a word, why—
you can make any laws you like.

JOHN BEAL

But Hussein is king here; he is Lord of the
Pass, and that's everything here. I'm nobody.

MIRALDA

O, if you like to be nobody, of course that's
different.

IF

ARCHIE BEAL

I think she means that if Hussein weren't
there there'd be only you. Of course, I don't
know. I've only just come.

JOHN BEAL

But we can't kill Hussein!

[MIRALDA *begins to cry.*]

O Lord! Good heavens! Please, Miss
Clement! I'm awfully sorry if I've said anything you didn't like. I wouldn't do that for
worlds. I'm awfully sorry. It's a beastly
country, I know. I'm really sorry you came.
I feel it's all my fault. I'm really awfully
sorry. . . .

MIRALDA

Never mind. Never mind. I was so helpless, and I asked you to help me. I never
ought to have done it. I oughtn't to have
spoken to you at all in that train without
being introduced; but I was so helpless. And
now, and now, I haven't a penny in the world,
and, O, I don't know what to do.

ARCHIE BEAL

We'll do anything for you, Miss Clement.

JOHN BEAL

Anything in the wide world. Please, please
don't cry. We'll do anything.

IF

MIRALDA

I . . . I only, I only wanted to—to kill
Hussein. But never mind, it doesn't matter
now.

JOHN BEAL

We'll do it, Miss Clement, won't we,
Archie? Only don't cry. We'll do it. I—I
suppose he deserves it, doesn't he?

ARCHIE BEAL

Yes, I suppose he does.

JOHN BEAL

Well, all right, Miss Clement, that's settled.
My brother and I will talk it over.

MIRALDA [*still sniffing*]

And—and—don't hang him or anything—
he looks so fine. . . . I—I wouldn't like
him treated like that. He has such a grand
beard. He ought to die fighting.

JOHN BEAL

We'll see what we can do, Miss Clement.

MIRALDA

It is sweet of you. It's really sweet. It's
sweet of both of you. I don't know what I'd
have done without you. I seemed to know
it that day the moment I saw you.

IF

JOHN BEAL

O, it's nothing, Miss Clement, nothing at all.

ARCHIE BEAL

That's all right.

MIRALDA

Well, now I'll have to look for an hotel.

JOHN BEAL

Yes, that's the trouble, that really is the trouble. That's what I've been thinking of all the time.

MIRALDA

Why; isn't there . . .

JOHN BEAL

No, I'm afraid there isn't. What are we to do, Archie.

ARCHIE BEAL

I—I can't think. Perhaps Miss Clement would have a scheme.

MIRALDA [to JOHN BEAL]

I rely on you, Mr. Beal.

JOHN BEAL

I—I; but what can I . . . You see, you're all alone. If you'd anyone with you, you could have . . .

IF

MIRALDA

I did think of bringing a rather nice aunt.
But on the whole I thought it better not to
tell anyone.

JOHN BEAL

Not to tell . . .

MIRALDA

No, on the whole I didn't.

JOHN BEAL

I say, Archie, what are we to do?

ARCHIE BEAL

Here's Daoud.

[*Enter* DAOUD.]

JOHN BEAL

The one man I trust in Al Shaldomir!

DAOUD

I have brought two watchers of the doorstep to guard the noble lady.

JOHN BEAL

He says he's brought two watchers of the
doorstep to look after Miss Clement.

ARCHIE BEAL

Two chaperons! Splendid! She can go
anywhere now.

IF

JOHN BEAL

Well, really, that is better. Yes that will be all right. We can find a room for you now. The trouble was your being alone. I hope you'll like them. [*To* DAOUD.] Tell them to enter here.

DAOUD [*beckoning in the doorway*]

Ho! Enter!

JOHN BEAL

That's all right, Archie, isn't it?

ARCHIE BEAL

Yes, that's all right. A chaperon's a chaperon, black or white.

JOHN BEAL

You won't mind their being black, will you, Miss Clement?

MIRALDA

No, I shan't mind. They can't be worse than white ones.

[*Enter* BAZZALOL *and* THOOTHOOBABA, *two enormous Nubians, bearing peacock fans and wearing scimitars. All stare at them. They begin to fan slightly.*]

DAOUD

The watchers of the doorstep.

110

IF

JOHN BEAL

Idiot, Daoud! Fools! Dolts! Men may not guard a lady's door.

[BAZZALOL *and* THOOTHOOBABA *smile ingratiatingly.*]

BAZZALOL [*bowing*]

We are not men.

Curtain

Six and a half years elapse

THE SONG OF THE IRIS MARSHES

When morn is bright on the mountains olden
   Till dawn is lost in the blaze of day,
When morn is bright and the marshes golden,
   Where shall the lost lights fade away?
   And where, my love, shall we dream to-day?

Dawn is fled to the marshy hollows
   Where ghosts of stars in the dimness stray,
And the water is streaked with the flash of
      swallows
   And all through summer the iris sway.
   But where, my love, shall we dream to-day?

When night is black in the iris marshes.

ACT III

Six and a half years later.
Al Shaldomir.
A room in the palace.
MIRALDA *reclines on a heap of cushions.*
JOHN *beside her.*
Bazzalol and Thoothoobaba fan them.

OMAR [*declaiming to a zither*]

Al Shaldomir, Al Shaldomir,
  The nightingales that guard thy ways
Cease not to give thee, after God
  And after Paradise, all praise.
Thou art the theme of all their lays.

Al Shaldomir, Al Shaldomir. . . ,

MIRALDA

Go now, Omar.

OMAR

O lady, I depart.
   [*Exit.*]

115

IF

MIRALDA [*languidly*]

John, John. I wish you'd marry me.

JOHN

Miralda, you're thinking of those old customs again that we left behind us seven years ago. What's the good of it?

MIRALDA

I had a fancy that I wished you would.

JOHN

What's the good of it? You know you are my beloved. There are none of those clergymen within hundreds of miles. What's the good of it?

MIRALDA

We could find one, John.

JOHN

O, yes, I suppose we could, but . . .

MIRALDA

Why won't you?

JOHN

I told you why.

MIRALDA

O, yes, that instinct that you must not marry. That's not your reason, John.

116

IF

JOHN

Yes, it is.

MIRALDA

It's a silly reason. It's a crazy reason. It's no reason at all. There's some other reason.

JOHN

No, there isn't. But I feel that in my bones. I don't know why. You know that I love none else but you. Besides, we're never going back, and it doesn't matter. This isn't Blackheath.

MIRALDA

So I must live as your slave.

JOHN

No, no, Miralda. My dear, you are not my slave. Did not the singer compare our love to the desire of the nightingale for the evening star? All know that you are my queen.

MIRALDA

They do not know at home.

JOHN

Home? Home? How could they know? What have we in common with home? Rows and rows of little houses; and if they hear a

117

nightingale there they write to the papers.
And—and if they saw this they'd think they
were drunk. Miralda, don't be absurd.
What has set you thinking of home?

MIRALDA

I want to be crowned queen.

JOHN

But I am not a king. I am only Shereef.

MIRALDA

You are all-powerful here, John, you can do
what you please, if you wish to. You don't
love me at all.

JOHN

Miralda, you know I love you. Didn't
I kill Hussein for you?

MIRALDA

Yes, but you don't love me now.

JOHN

And Hussein's people killed Archie. That
was for you too. I brought my brother out
here to help you. He was engaged to be
married, too.

MIRALDA

But you don't love me now.

IF

JOHN

Yes, I do. I love you as the dawn loves the iris marshes. You know the song they sing.[1]

MIRALDA

Then why won't you marry me?

JOHN

I told you, I told you. I had a dream about the future. I forgot the dream, but I know I was not to marry. I will not wrong the future.

MIRALDA

Don't be crazy.

JOHN

I will have what fancies I please, crazy or sane. Am I not Shereef of Shaldomir? Who dare stop me if I would be mad as Herod?

MIRALDA

I will be crowned queen.

JOHN

It is not my wish.

MIRALDA

I will, I will, I will.

[1] See p. 113.

119

IF

JOHN

Drive me not to anger. If I have you cast into a well and take twenty of the fairest daughters of Al Shaldomir in your place, who can gainsay me?

MIRALDA

I will be crowned queen.

JOHN

O, do not be tiresome.

MIRALDA

Was it not my money that brought you here? Was it not I who said "Kill Hussein"? What power could you have had, had Hussein lived? What would you have been doing now, but for me?

JOHN

I don't know, Miralda.

MIRALDA

Catching some silly train to the City. Working for some dull firm. Living in some small suburban house. It is I, *I*, that brought you from all that, and you won't make me a queen.

JOHN

Is it not enough that you are my beloved? You know there is none other but you. Is it not enough, Miralda?

IF

MIRALDA

It is not enough. I will be queen.

JOHN

Tchah! . . . Miralda, I know you are a
wonderful woman, the most wonderful in the
East; how you ever came to be in the West
I don't know, and a train of all places; but,
Miralda, you must not have petty whims,
they don't become you.

MIRALDA

Is it a petty whim to wish to be a queen?

JOHN

Yes, when it is only the name you want.
You *are* a queen. You have all you wish for.
Are you not my beloved? And have I not
power here over all men? Could I not close
the pass?

MIRALDA

I want to be queen.

JOHN

Oh-h! I will leave you. I have more to do
than to sit and hear your whims. When I
come back you will have some other whim.
Miralda, you have too many whims.

[*He rises.*]

121

IF

MIRALDA

Will you be back soon?

JOHN

No.

MIRALDA

When will you come back, John?

[*She is reclining, looking fair, fanning slightly.*]

JOHN

In half an hour.

MIRALDA

In half an hour?

JOHN

Yes.

[*Exit.*]

MIRALDA

Half an hour.

[*Her fan is laid down. She clutches it with sudden resolve. She goes to the wall, fanning herself slowly. She leans against it. She fans herself now with obvious deliberation. Three times the great fan goes flat against the window, and then again separately three times; and then she puts it against the window once*

with a smile of ecstasy. She has signalled.
She returns to the cushions and reclines
with beautiful care, fanning herself softly.

Enter the Vizier, HAFIZ EL ALCOLAHN]

HAFIZ

Lady! You bade me come.

MIRALDA

Did I, Hafiz?

HAFIZ

Lady, your fan.

MIRALDA

Ah, I was fanning myself.

HAFIZ

Seven times, lady.

MIRALDA

Ah, was it? Well, now you're here . . .

HAFIZ

Lady, O star of these times. O light over
lonely marshes. [*He kneels by her and em-*
braces her.] Is the Shereef gone, lady?

MIRALDA

For half an hour, Hafiz.

123

IF

HAFIZ

How know you for half an hour?

MIRALDA

He said so.

HAFIZ

He said so? Then is the time to fear, if a man say so.

MIRALDA

I know him.

HAFIZ

In our country who knows any man so much? None.

MIRALDA

He'll be away for half an hour.

HAFIZ [*embracing*]

O, exquisite lily of unattainable mountains.

MIRALDA

Ah, Hafiz, would you do a little thing for me?

HAFIZ

I would do all things, lady, O evening star.

IF

MIRALDA

Would you make me a queen, Hafiz?

HAFIZ

If—if the Shereef were gathered?

MIRALDA

Even so, Hafiz.

HAFIZ

Lady, I would make you queen of all that
lies west of the passes.

MIRALDA

You would make me queen?

HAFIZ

Indeed, before all my wives, before all
women, over all Shaldomir, named the elect.

MIRALDA

O, well, Hafiz; then you may kiss me.
[HAFIZ *does so ad lib.*]
Hafiz, the Shereef has irked me.

HAFIZ

Lady, O singing star, to all men is the hour.

125

IF

MIRALDA

The appointed hour?

HAFIZ

Even the appointed hour, the last, leading to darkness.

MIRALDA

Is it written, think you, that the Shereef's hour is soon?

HAFIZ

Lady, O dawn's delight, let there be a banquet. Let the great ones of Shaldomir be bidden there.

MIRALDA

There shall be a banquet, Hafiz.

HAFIZ

Soon, O lady. Let it be soon, sole lily of the garden.

MIRALDA

It shall be soon, Hafiz.

[*More embraces.*]

And above all, O lady, bid Daoud, the son of the baker.

MIRALDA

He shall be bidden, Hafiz.

IF

HAFIZ

O lady, it is well.

MIRALDA

Go now, Hafiz.

HAFIZ

Lady, I go [*giving a bag of gold to* BAZZALOL].
Silence. Silence. Silence.

BAZZALOL [*kneeling*]

O, master!

HAFIZ

Let the tomb speak; let the stars cry out;
but do you be silent.

BAZZALOL

Aye, master.

HAFIZ [*to* THOOTHOOBABA]

And you. Though this one speak, yet be
silent, or dread the shadow of Hafiz el Alcolahn.

> [*He drops a bag of gold.* THOOTHOO-
> BABA *goes down and grabs at the gold;
> his eyes gloat over it.*]

THOOTHOOBABA

Master, I speak not. Oh-h-h.

[*Exit* HAFIZ.

IF

MIRALDA *arranges herself on the cush-*
ions. She looks idly at each Nubian. The
Nubians put each a finger over his lips and
go on fanning with one hand.]

MIRALDA

A queen. I shall look sweet as a queen.
[*Enter* JOHN. *She rises to greet him*
caressingly.
Enter DAOUD.]
Oh, you have brought Daoud with you.

JOHN

Why not?

MIRALDA

You know that I don't like Daoud.

JOHN

I wish to speak with him.
[MIRALDA *looks straight at* JOHN *and*
moves away in silence. Exit L.]

JOHN

Daoud.

DAOUD

Great master.

JOHN

Daoud, one day in spring, in the cemetery
of those called Blessed, beyond the city's

128

gates, you swore to me by the graves of both
your parents . . .

DAOUD

Great master, even so I swore.

JOHN

. . . to be true to me always.

DAOUD

There is no Shereef but my master.

JOHN

Daoud, you have kept your word.

DAOUD

I have sought to, master.

JOHN

You have helped me often, Daoud, warned
me and helped me often. Through you I
knew those currents that run through the
deeps of the market, in silence and all men
feel them, but a ruler never. You told me of
them, and when I knew—then I could look
after myself, Daoud. They could do nothing
against me then. Well, now I hold this
people. I hold them at last, Daoud, and now
—well, I can rest a little.

DAOUD

Not in the East, master.

IF

JOHN

Not in the East, Daoud?

DAOUD

No, master.

JOHN

Why? What do you mean?

DAOUD

In Western countries, master, whose tales I have read, in a wonderful book named the "Good Child's History of England," in the West a man hath power over a land, and lo! the power is his and descends to his son's son after him.

JOHN

Well, doesn't it in the East?

DAOUD

Not if he does not watch, master; in the night and the day, and in the twilight between the day and the night, and in the dawn between the night and the day.

JOHN

I thought you had pretty long dynasties in these parts, and pretty lazy ones.

IF

DAOUD

Master, he that was mightiest of those that
were kings in Babylon had a secret door prepared in an inner chamber, which led to a
little room, the smallest in the palace, whose
back door opened secretly to the river, even
to great Euphrates, where a small boat waited
all the days of his reign.

JOHN

Did he really now? Well, *he* was taking no
chances. Did he have to use it?

DAOUD

No, master. Such boats are never used.
Those that watch like that do not need to
seek them, and the others, they would never
be able to reach the river in time, even though
the boat were there.

JOHN

I shouldn't like to have to live like that.
Why, a river runs by the back of this palace.
I suppose palaces usually are on rivers. I'm
glad I don't have to keep a boat there.

DAOUD

No, master.

JOHN

Well, what is it you are worrying about?
Who is it you are afraid of?

IF

DAOUD

Hafiz el Alcolahn.

JOHN

O, Hafiz. I have no fears of Hafiz. Lately
I ordered my spies to watch him no longer.
Why does he hate me?

DAOUD

Because, most excellent master, you slew
Hussein.

JOHN

Slew Hussein? What is that to do with
him? May I not slay whom I please?

DAOUD

Even so, master. Even so. But he was
Hussein's enemy.

JOHN

His enemy, eh?

DAOUD

For years he had dreamed of the joy of
killing Hussein.

JOHN

Well, he should have done it before I came.
We don't hang over things and brood over

132

IF

them for years where I come from. If a
thing's to be done, it's done.

DAOUD

Even so, master. Hafiz had laid his plans
for years. He would have killed him and got
his substance; and then, when the hour drew
near, you came, and Hussein died, swiftly,
not as Hafiz would have had him die; and
lo! thou art the lord of the pass, and Hafiz is
no more than a beetle that runs about in the
dirt.

JOHN

Well, so you fear Hafiz?

DAOUD

Not for himself, master. Nay, I fear not
Hafiz. But, master, hast thou seen when the
thunder is coming, but no rumble is heard,
and the sky is scarce yet black, how little
winds run in the grass and sigh and die; and
the flower beckons a moment with its head;
all the world full of whispers, master, all saying nothing; then the lightning, master, and
the anger of God; and men say it came without warning? [*Simply.*] I hear those things
coming, master.

JOHN

Well?

133

IF

DAOUD

Master, it is all silent in the market. Once, when the price of turquoises was high, men abused the Shereef. When the merchant men could not sell their pomegranates for silver they abused the Shereef. It is men's way, master, men's way. Now it is all silent in the market. It is like the grasses with the little winds, that whisper and sigh and die away; like the flowers beckoning to nothing. And so, master, and so . . .

JOHN

I see, you fear some danger.

DAOUD

I fear it, master.

JOHN

What danger, Daoud?

DAOUD

Master, I know not.

JOHN

From what quarter, Daoud?

DAOUD

O master, O sole Lord of Al Shaldomir, named the elect, from that quarter.

IF

JOHN

That quarter? Why, that is the gracious lady's innermost chamber.

DAOUD

From that quarter, great master, O Lord of the Pass.

JOHN

Daoud, I have cast men into prison for saying less than this. Men have been flogged on the feet for less than this.

DAOUD

Slay me, master, but hear my words.

JOHN

I will not slay you. You are mistaken, Daoud. You have made a great mistake. The thing is absurd. Why, the gracious lady has scarcely seen Hafiz. She knows nothing of the talk of the market. Who could tell her? No one comes here. It is absurd. Only the other day she said to me . . . But it is absurd, it is absurd, Daoud. Besides, the people would never rebel against me. Do I not govern them well?

DAOUD

Even so, master.

IF

JOHN

Why should they rebel, then?

DAOUD

They think of the old times, master.

JOHN

The old times? Why, their lives weren't safe. The robbers came down from the mountains and robbed the market whenever they had a mind.

DAOUD

Master, men were content in the old times.

JOHN

But were the merchants content?

DAOUD

Those that loved merchandise were content, master. Those that loved it not went into the mountains.

JOHN

But were they content when they were robbed?

DAOUD

They soon recovered their losses, master. Their prices were unjust and they loved usury.

IF

JOHN

And were the people content with unjust prices?

DAOUD

Some were, master, as men have to be in all countries. The others went into the mountains and robbed the merchants.

JOHN

I see.

DAOUD

But now, master, a man robs a merchant and he is cast into prison. Now a man is slain in the market and his son, his own son, master, may not follow after the aggressor and slay him and burn his house. They are ill-content, master. No man robs the merchants, no man slays them, and the merchants' hearts are hardened and they oppress all men.

JOHN

I see. They don't like good government?

DAOUD

They sigh for the old times, master.

JOHN

I see; I see. In spite of all I have done for them, they want their old bad government back again.

IF

DAOUD

It is the old way, master.

JOHN

Yes, yes. And so they would rebel. Well, we must watch. You have warned me once again, Daoud, and I am grateful. But you are wrong, Daoud, about the gracious lady. You are mistaken. It is impossible. You are mistaken, Daoud. I know it could not be.

DAOUD

I am mistaken, master. Indeed, I am mistaken. Yet, watch. Watch, master.

JOHN

Well, I will watch.

DAOUD

And, master, if ever I come to you bearing oars, then watch no longer, master, but follow me through the banquet chamber and through the room beyond it. Move as the wild deer move when there is danger, without pausing, without wondering, without turning round; for in that hour, master, in that hour . . .

JOHN

Through the room beyond the banquet chamber, Daoud?

138

IF

DAOUD

Aye, master, following me.

JOHN

But there is no door beyond, Daoud.

DAOUD

Master, I have prepared a door.

JOHN

A door, Daoud?

DAOUD

A door none wots of, master.

JOHN

Whither does it lead?

DAOUD

To a room that you know not of, a little room; you must stoop, master.

JOHN

O, and then?

DAOUD

To the river, master.

JOHN

The river! But there's no boat there.

139

IF

DAOUD

Under the golden willow, master.

JOHN

A boat?

DAOUD

Even so, under the branches.

JOHN

Is it come to that? . . . No, Daoud, all this is unnecessary. It can't come to that.

DAOUD

If ever I come before you bearing two oars, in that hour, master, it is necessary.

JOHN

But you will not come. It will never come to that.

DAOUD

No, master.

JOHN

A wise man can stop things before they get as far as that.

DAOUD

They that were kings in Babylon were wise men, master.

140

IF

JOHN

Babylon! But that was thousands of years ago.

DAOUD

Man changes not, master.

JOHN

Well, Daoud, I will trust you, and if it ever comes to that . . .

[*Enter* MIRALDA.]

MIRALDA

I thought Daoud was gone.

DAOUD

Even now I go, gracious lady.

[*Exit* DAOUD. *Rather strained silence with* JOHN *and* MIRALDA *till he goes. She goes and makes herself comfortable on the cushions. He is not entirely at ease.*]

MIRALDA

You had a long talk with Daoud.

JOHN

Yes, he came and talked a good deal.

MIRALDA

What about?

141

IF

John

O, just talk; you know these Eastern people.

Miralda

I thought it was something you were discussing with him.

John

O, no.

Miralda

Some important secret.

John

No, not at all.

Miralda

You often talk with Daoud.

John

Yes, he is useful to me.   When he talks sense I listen, but to-day . . .

Miralda

What did he come for to-day?

John

O, nothing.

142

IF

MIRALDA

You have a secret with Daoud that you
will not share with me.

JOHN

No, I have not.

MIRALDA

What was it he said?

JOHN

He said there was a king in Babylon who
. . .

[DAOUD *slips into the room.*]

MIRALDA

In Babylon? What has that to do with
us?

JOHN

Nothing. I told you he was not talking
sense.

MIRALDA

Well, what did he say?

JOHN

He said that in Babylon . . .

143

IF

DAOUD

Hist!

JOHN

O, well . . .

[MIRALDA *glares, but calms herself and says nothing.*

Exit DAOUD.]

MIRALDA

What did Daoud say of Babylon?

JOHN

O, well, as you say, it had nothing to do with us.

MIRALDA

But I wish to hear it.

JOHN

I forget.

[*For a moment there is silence.*]

MIRALDA

John, John. Will you do a little thing for me?

JOHN

What is it?

144

IF

MIRALDA

Say you will do it, John. I should love to have one of my little wishes granted.

JOHN

What is it?

MIRALDA

Kill Daoud, John. I want you to kill Daoud.

JOHN

I will not.

[*He walks up and down in front of the two Nubians in silence. She plucks petulantly at a pillow. She suddenly calms herself. A light comes into her eyes. The Nubians go on fanning.* JOHN *goes on pacing.*]

MIRALDA

John, John, I have forgotten my foolish fancies.

JOHN

I am glad of it.

MIRALDA

I do not really wish you to kill Daoud.

JOHN [*same voice*]

I'm glad you don't.

IF

MIRALDA

I have only one fancy now, John.

JOHN

Well, what is it?

MIRALDA

Give a banquet, John. I want you to give
a banquet.

JOHN

A banquet? Why?

MIRALDA

Is there any harm in my fancy?

JOHN

No.

MIRALDA

Then if I may not be a queen, and if you
will not kill Daoud for me, give a banquet,
John. There is no harm in a banquet.

JOHN

Very well. When do you want it?

MIRALDA

To-morrow, John. Bid all the great ones
to it, all the illustrious ones in Al Shaldomir.

IF

JOHN

Very well.

MIRALDA

And bid Daoud come.

JOHN

Daoud? You asked me to kill him.

MIRALDA

I do not wish that any longer, John.

JOHN

You have queer moods, Miralda.

MIRALDA

May I not change my moods, John?

JOHN

I don't know. I don't understand them.

MIRALDA

And ask Hafiz el Alcolahn, John.

JOHN

Hafiz? Why?

MIRALDA

I don't know, John. It was just my fancy.

147

IF

JOHN
Your fancy, eh?

MIRALDA
That was all.

JOHN
Then I will ask him. Have you any other fancy?

MIRALDA
Not now, John.

JOHN
Then go, Miralda.

MIRALDA
Go?

JOHN
Yes.

MIRALDA
Why?

JOHN
Because I command it.

MIRALDA
Because you command it?

JOHN
Yes, I, the Shereef Al Shaldomir.

IF

MIRALDA

Very well.

[*Exit L.*

*He walks to the door to see that she is
really gone. He comes back to centre and
stands with back to audience, pulling a
cord quietly from his pocket and arranging
it.*

He moves half left and comes up behind
BAZZALOL. *Suddenly he slips the cord
over* BAZZALOL'S *head, and tightens it
round his neck.*]

[BAZZALOL *flops on his knees.*

THOOTHOOBABA *goes on fanning.*]

JOHN

Speak!

[BAZZALOL *is silent.*

JOHN *tightens it more.* THOOTHOOBABA
goes on quietly fanning.]

BAZZALOL

I cannot.

JOHN

If you would speak, raise your left hand.
If you raise your left hand and do not speak
you shall die·

IF

[BAZZALOL *is silent.* JOHN *tightens more.* BAZZALOL *raises his great flabby left hand high.* JOHN *releases the cord.* BAZZALOL *blinks and moves his mouth.*]

BAZZALOL

Gracious Shereef, one visited the great lady and gave us gold, saying, "Speak not."

JOHN

When?

BAZZALOL

Great master, one hour since.

JOHN [*a little viciously*]

Who?

BAZZALOL

O heaven-sent, he was Hafiz el Alcolahn.

JOHN

Give me the gold.

[BAZZALOL *gives it.*]

[*To* THOOTHOOBABA.] Give me the gold.

THOOTHOOBABA

Master, none gave me gold.

[JOHN *touches his dagger, and looks like using it.*

THOOTHOOBABA *gives it.*]

IF

John

Take back your gold. Be silent about this.
You too.

[*He throws gold to* Bazzalol.]

Gold does not make you silent, but there is
a thing that does. What is that thing?
Speak. What thing makes you silent?

Bazzalol

O, great master, it is death.

John

Death, eh? And how will you die if you
speak? You know how you will die?

Bazzalol

Yes, heaven-sent.

John

Tell your comrade, then.

Bazzalol

We shall be eaten, great master.

John

You know by what?

BAZZALOL

Small things, great master, small things.
Oh-h-h-h. Oh-h-h.

[THOOTHOOBABA'S *knees scarcely hold
him.*]

JOHN

It is well.

Curtain

SCENE 2

*A small street. Al Shaldomir.
Time: Next day.*

[*Enter L. the* SHEIK OF THE BISHAR-
EENS.

*He goes to an old green door, pointed of
course in the Arabic way.*]

SHEIK OF THE BISHAREENS

Ho, Bishareens!

[*The* BISHAREENS *run on.*]

SHEIK

It is the place and the hour.

BISHAREENS

Ah, ah!

152

IF

SHEIK [*to* FIRST BISHAREEN]
Watch.

   [FIRST BISHAREEN *goes to right and
watches up sunny street.*]

FIRST BISHAREEN
He comes.

   [*Enter* HAFIZ EL ALCOLAHN. *He goes
straight up to the* SHEIK *and whispers.*]

SHEIK [*turning*]
Hear, O Bishareens.

   [HAFIZ *places flute to his lips.*]

A BISHAREEN
And the gold, master?

SHEIK
Silence! It is the signal.

   [HAFIZ *plays a weird, strange tune on
his flute.*]

HAFIZ
So.

SHEIK
Master, once more.

   [HAFIZ *raises the flute again to his lips.*]

153

IF

SHEIK

Hear, O Bishareens!

[*He plays the brief tune again.*]

HAFIZ [*to* SHEIK]

Like that.

SHEIK

We have heard, O master.

[*He walks away L. Hands move in the direction of knife-hilts.*]

THE BISHAREENS

Ah, ah!

[*Exit* HAFIZ.

He plays a merry little tune on his flute as he walks away.]

Curtain

SCENE 3

The banqueting hall. A table along the back. JOHN *and* MIRALDA *seated with notables of Al Shaldomir.*

JOHN *sits in the centre, with* MIRALDA *on his right and, next to her,* HAFIZ EL ALCOLAHN.

154

IF

MIRALDA [*to* JOHN]
You bade Daoud be present?

JOHN
Yes.

MIRALDA
He is not here.

JOHN
Daoud not here?

MIRALDA
No.

JOHN
Why?

MIRALDA
We all obey you, but not Daoud.

JOHN
I do not understand it.

A NOTABLE
The Shereef has frowned.

    [*Enter R. an* OFFICER-AT-ARMS. *He halts at once and salutes with his sword, then takes a side pace to his left, standing against the wall, sword at the carry.*

    JOHN *acknowledges salute by touching his forehead with the inner tips of his fingers.*]

155

IF

OFFICER-AT-ARMS

Soldiers of Al Shaldomir; with the dance-step; march.

[*Enter R. some men in single file; uniform, pale green silks; swords at carry. They advance in single file, in a slightly serpentine way, deviating to their left a little out of the straight and returning to it, stepping neatly on the tips of their toes. Their march is fantastic and odd without being exactly funny.*

The OFFICER-AT-ARMS *falls in on their left flank and marches about level with the third or fourth man.*

When he reaches the centre he gives another word of command.]

OFFICER-AT-ARMS

With reverence: Salute.

[*The actor who takes this part should have been an officer or N. C. O.*

JOHN *stands up and acknowledges their salute by touching his forehead with the fingers of the right hand, palm turned inwards.*

Exeunt soldiers L. JOHN *sits down.*]

A NOTABLE

He does not smile this evening.

156

IF

A WOMAN

The Shereef?

NOTABLE

He has not smiled.

[*Enter R.* ZABNOOL, *a* CONJURER, *with brass bowl. He bows. He walks to centre opposite* JOHN. *He exhibits his bowl.*]

ZABNOOL

Behold. The bowl is empty.

[ZABNOOL *produces a snake.*]

ZABNOOL

Ah, little servant of Death.

[*He produces flowers.*]

Flowers, master, flowers. All the way from Nowhere.

[*He produces birds.*]

Birds, master. Birds from Nowhere. Sing, sing to the Shereef. Sing the little empty songs of the land of Nowhere.

[*He seats himself on the ground facing* JOHN. *He puts the bowl on the ground. He places a piece of silk, with queer designs on it, over the bowl. He partly draws the silk away with his left hand and puts in his right. He brings out a young crocodile and holds it by the neck.*]

157

IF

CONJURER

Behold, O Shereef; O people, behold; a crocodile.

[*He arises and bows to* JOHN *and wraps up the crocodile in some drapery and walks away. As he goes he addresses his crocodile.*]

O eater of lambs, O troubler of the rivers, you sought to evade me in an empty bowl. O thief, O appetite, you sought to evade the Shereef. The Shereef has seen you, O vexer of swimmers, O pig in armour, O . . .

[*Exit.*

SHABEESH, *another* CONJURER, *rushes on.*]

SHABEESH

Bad man, master; he very, very bad man.

[*He pushes* ZABNOOL *away roughly, impetus of which carries* ZABNOOL *to the wings.*]

Very, very bad man, master.

MIRALDA [*reprovingly*]

Zabnool has amused us.

SHABEESH

He very, very bad man, lily lady. He get crocodile from devil. From devil Poolyana, lily lady. Very, very bad.

IF

MIRALDA

He may call on devils if he amuse us,
Shabeesh.

SHABEESH

But Poolyana, *my* devil. He call on *my*
devil, lily lady. Very, very, very bad. My
devil Poolyana.

MIRALDA

Call on him yourself, Shabeesh. Amuse
us.

SHABEESH

Shall one devil serve two masters?

MIRALDA

Why not?

SHABEESH [*beginning to wave priestly conjurer's
hands*]

Very bad man go away. Go away, bad
man: go away, bad man. Poolyana not want
bad man: Poolyana only work for good man.
He mighty fine devil. Poolyana, Poolyana.
Big, black, fine, furry devil. Poolyana, Poolyana, Poolyana. O fine, fat devil with big
angry tail. Poolyana, Poolyana, Poolyana.
Send me up fine young pig for the Shereef.
Poolyana, Poolyana. Lil yellow pig with
curly tail. [*Small pig appears.*] O Pooly-

IF

ana, great Poolyana. Fine black fur and grey fur underneath. Fine ferocious devil, you *my* devil, Poolyana. O, Poolyana, Poolyana, Poolyana. Send me a big beast what chew bad man's crocodile. Big beast with big teeth, eat him like a worm.

[*He has spread large silk handkerchief on floor and is edging back from it in alarm.*]

Long nails in him toes, big like lion, Poolyana. Send great smelly big beast—eat up bad man's crocodile.

[*At first stir of handkerchief* SHABEESH *leaps in alarm.*]

He come, he come. I see his teeth and horns.

[*Enter small live rabbit from trapdoor under handkerchief.*]

O, Poolyana, you big devil have your liddle joke. You laugh at poor conjuring man. You send him lil rabbit to eat big crocodile. Bad Poolyana. Bad Poolyana.

[*Whacks ground with stick.*]
You plenty bad devil, Poolyana.

[*Whacking it again. Handkerchief has been thrown on ground again. Handkerchief stirs slightly.*]

No, no, Poolyana. You not bad devil. You not bad devil. You plenty good devil. Poolyana. No, no, no! Poor conjuring man

160

quite happy on muddy earth. No, Poolyana,
no! O, no, no, devil. O, no, no! Hell plenty
nice place for devil. Master! He not my
devil! He other man's devil!

JOHN

What's this noise? What's it about?
What's the matter?

SHABEESH [*in utmost terror*]

He coming, master! Coming!

ZABNOOL

Poolyana, Poolyana, Poolyana. Stay
down, stay down, Poolyana. Stay down in
nice warm hell, Poolyana. The Shereef want
no devil to-day.

[ZABNOOL *before speaking returns to
centre and pats air over ground where
handkerchief lies.*

Then SHABEESH *and* ZABNOOL *come
together side by side and bow and smile
together toward the* SHEREEF. *Gold is
thrown to them, which* ZABNOOL *gathers
and hands to* SHABEESH, *who gives a share
back to* ZABNOOL.]

A NOTABLE

The Shereef is silent.

[*Enter three women R. in single file,
dancing, and carrying baskets full of pink
rose-leaves. They dance across, throwing*

IF

*down rose-leaves, leaving a path of them
behind them.   Exeunt L.*]

A NOTABLE

Still he is silent.

MIRALDA

Why do you not speak?

JOHN

I do not wish to speak.

MIRALDA

Why?

[*Enter* OMAR *with his zither.*]

OMAR [*singing*]

Al Shaldomir, Al Shaldomir,
  Birds sing thy praises night and day;
The nightingale in every wood,
  Blackbirds in fields profound with may;
  Birds sing of thee by every way.

Al Shaldomir, Al Shaldomir,
  My heart is ringing with thee still;
Though far away, O fairy fields,
  My soul flies low by every hill
  And misses not one daffodil.

Al Shaldomir, Al Shaldomir,
  O mother of my roving dreams,
Blue is the night above thy spires,
  And blue by myriads of streams,
  Paradise through thy gateway gleams.

162

IF

MIRALDA

Why do you not wish to speak?

JOHN

You desire me to speak?

MIRALDA

No. They all wonder why you do not speak; that is all.

JOHN

I will speak. They shall hear me.

MIRALDA

O, there is no need to.

JOHN

There *is* a need. [*He rises.*] People of Shaldomir, behold I know your plottings. I know the murmurings that you murmur against me. When I sleep in my inner chamber my ear is in the market, while I sit at meat I hear men whisper far hence and know their innermost thoughts. Hope not to overcome me by your plans nor by any manner of craftiness. My gods are gods of brass; none have escaped them. They cannot be overthrown. Of all men they favour my people. Their hands reach out to the uttermost ends of the earth. Take heed, for my gods are terrible. I am the Shereef; if any dare withstand me I will call on my gods and they shall crush him utterly. They shall grind him into the earth and trample him under, as though he had not been. The uttermost parts have feared the gods of the English. They reach out, they destroy, there is no escape from them. Be warned; for I do not permit any to stand against me. The laws that I have given you, you shall keep; there shall be no other laws. Whoso murmurs shall know my wrath and the wrath of my gods. Take heed, I speak not twice. I spoke once to Hussein. Hussein heard not; and Hussein is dead; his ears are closed for ever. Hear, O people.

HAFIZ

O Shereef, we murmur not against you.

JOHN

I know thoughts and hear whispers. I need not instruction, Hafiz.

HAFIZ

You exalt yourself over us as none did aforetime.

JOHN

Yes. And I will exalt myself. I have been Shereef hitherto, but now I will be king. Al Shaldomir is less than I desire. I have ruled too long over a little country. I will be the equal of Persia. I will be king; I proclaim it. The pass is mine; the mountains shall be mine also. And he that rules the mountains has mastery over all the plains beyond. If the men of the plains will not own it let them make ready; for my wrath will fall on them in the hour when they think me afar, on a night when they think I dream. I proclaim myself king over . . .

[HAFIZ *pulls out his flute and plays the weird, strange tune.* JOHN *looks at him in horrified anger.*]

JOHN

The penalty is death! Death is the punishment for what you do, Hafiz. You have dared while I spoke. Hafiz, your contempt is death. Go to Hussein. I, the king . . . say it.

[DAOUD *has entered R., bearing two oars.* DAOUD *walks across, not looking at* JOHN. *Exit by small door in L. near back.*

JOHN *gives one look at the banqueters, then he follows* DAOUD. *Exit.*

All look astonished. Some rise and peer. HAFIZ *draws his knife.*]

OMAR [*singing*]

Al Shaldomir, Al Shaldomir,
    The nightingales that guard thy ways
Cease not to give thee, after God
And after Paradise, all praise,

IF

CRIES [*off*]

Kill the unbeliever. Kill the dog. Kill the Christian.

[*Enter the* SHEIK OF THE BISHAREENS, *followed by all his men.*]

SHEIK

We are the Bishareens, master.

[MIRALDA *standing up, right arm akimbo, left arm pointing perfectly straight out towards the small door, hand extended.*]

MIRALDA

He is there.

[*The* BISHAREENS *run off through the little door.*]

A NOTABLE

Not to interfere with old ways is wisest.

ANOTHER

Indeed, it would have been well for him.

[*The* BISHAREENS *begin to return looking all about them like disappointed hounds.*]

A BISHAREEN

He is not there, master.

HAFIZ

Not there? Not there? Why, there is no door beyond. He must needs be there, and his chief spy with him.

IF

SHEIK [*off*]

He is not here.

MIRALDA [*turning round and clawing the wall*]

O, I was weary of him. I was weary of him.

HAFIZ

Be comforted, pearl of the morning; he is gone.

MIRALDA

When I am weary of a man he must die.

[*He embraces her knees.*]

ZAGBOOLA [*who has come on with a little crowd that followed the* BISHAREENS. *She is blind.*]

Lead me to Hafiz. I am the mother of Hafiz. Lead me to Hafiz. [*They lead her near.*] Hafiz! Hafiz!

[*She finds his shoulder and tries to drag him away.*]

HAFIZ

Go! Go! I have found the sole pearl of the innermost deeps of the sea.

[*He is kneeling and kissing* MIRALDA'S *hand.* ZAGBOOLA *wails.*]

Curtain

ACT IV

Scene i

Three years elapse.

Scene: The street outside the Acacias.

Time: Evening.

[Ali leans on a pillar-box watching.

John shuffles on L. He is miserably dressed, an Englishman down on his luck.

A nightingale sings far off.]

JOHN

A nightingale here. Well, I never.

Al Shaldomir, Al Shaldomir,
  The nightingales that guard thy ways
Cease not to give thee, after God
  And after Paradise, all praise. . . .

The infernal place! I wish I had never seen it! Wonder what set me thinking of that?

> *[The nightingale sings another bar. JOHN turns to his left and walks down the little path that leads to the door of the Acacias.]*

168

IF

I mustn't come here. Mustn't come to a fine house like this. Mustn't. Mustn't.

[*He draws near it reluctantly. He puts his hand to the bell and withdraws it. Then he rings and snatches his hand away. He prepares to run away. Finally he rings it repeatedly, feverishly, violently.*

Enter LIZA, *opening the door.*]

LIZA

Ullo, 'Oo's this!

JOHN

I oughtn't to have rung, miss, I know. I oughtn't to have rung your bell; but I've seen better days, and wondered if—I wondred . . .

LIZA

I oughtn't to 'ave opened the door, that's wot *I* oughtn't. Now I look at you, I oughtn't to 'ave opened it. Wot does you want?

JOHN

O, don't turn me away now, miss. I must come here. I must.

LIZA

Must? Why?

JOHN

I don't know.

IF

LIZA

Wot do you want?

JOHN

Who lives here?

LIZA

Mr. and Mrs. Cater; firm of Briggs, Cater, and Johnstone. What do you want?

JOHN

Could I see Mr. Cater?

LIZA

He's out. Dining at the Mansion House.

JOHN

Oh.

LIZA

He is.

JOHN

Could I see Mrs. Cater?

LIZA

See Mrs. Cater? No, of course you couldn't.

[*She prepares to shut the door.*]

JOHN

Miss! Miss! Don't go, miss. Don't shut me out. If you knew what I'd suffered, if you knew what I'd suffered. Don't!

IF

LIZA [*coming forward again*]
Suffered? Why? Ain't you got enough to eat?

JOHN
No, I've had nothing all day.

LIZA
'Aven't you really now?

JOHN
No. And I get little enough at any time.

LIZA [*kindly*]
You ought to work.

JOHN
I . . . I can't. I can't bring myself . . .
I . . . I've seen better times.

LIZA
Still, you could work.

JOHN
I—I can't grub for halfpennies when I've
—when I've . . .

LIZA
When you've what?

JOHN
Lost millions.

IF

LIZA

Millions?

JOHN

I've lost everything.

LIZA

'Ow did you lose it?

JOHN

Through being blind. But never mind,
never mind. It's all gone now, and I'm
hungry.

LIZA

'Ow long 'ave you been down on your luck?

JOHN

It's three years now.

LIZA

Couldn't get a regular job, like?

JOHN

Well, I suppose I might have. I suppose
it's my fault, miss. But the heart was out of
me.

LIZA

Dear me, now

JOHN

Miss.

172

IF

LIZA

Yes?

JOHN

You've a kind face . . .

LIZA

'Ave I?

JOHN

Yes. Would you do me a kind turn?

LIZA

Well, I dunno. I might, as yer so down
on yer luck—I don't like to see a man like
you are, I must say.

JOHN

Would you let me come into the big house
and speak to the missus a moment?

LIZA

She'd row me awful if I did. This house is
very respectable.

JOHN

I feel, if you would, I feel, I feel my luck
might change.

LIZA

But I don't know what she'd say if I did.

JOHN

Miss, I must.

IF

LIZA

I don't know wot she'd say.

JOHN

I must come in, miss, I must.

LIZA

I don't know what she'll say.

JOHN

I must. I can't help myself.

LIZA

I don't know what she'll . . .

[JOHN *is in, door shuts.*]

[ALI *throws his head up and laughs, but quite silently.*]

Curtain

SCENE 2

The drawing-room at the Acacias.

A moment later.

The scene is the same as in Act I, except that the sofa which was red is now green, and the photograph of Aunt Martha is replaced by that of a frowning old colonel. The ages of the four children in the photo-

174

IF

graphs are the same, but their sexes have
changed.

[MARY *reading. Enter* LIZA.]

LIZA

There's a gentleman to see you, mum,
which is, properly speaking, not a gentleman
at all, but 'e would come in, mum.

MARY

Not a gentleman! Good gracious, Liza,
whatever do you mean?

'E would come in, mum.

MARY

But what does he want?

LIZA [*over shoulder*]

What does you want?

JOHN [*entering*]

I am a beggar.

MARY

O, really? You've no right to be coming
into houses like this, you know.

JOHN

I know that, madam, I know that. Yet
somehow I couldn't help myself. I've been
begging for nearly three years now, and I've

175

never done this before, yet somehow to-night I felt impelled to come to this house. I beg your pardon, humbly. Hunger drove me to it.

MARY

Hunger?

JOHN

I'm very hungry, madam.

MARY

Unfortunately Mr. Cater has not yet returned, or perhaps he might . . .

JOHN

If you could give me a little to eat yourself, madam, a bit of stale bread, a crust, something that Mr. Cater would not want.

MARY

It's very unusual, coming into a house like this and at such an hour—it's past eleven o'clock—and Mr. Cater not yet returned. Are you really hungry?

JOHN

I'm very, very hungry.

MARY

Well, it's very unusual; but perhaps I might get you a little something.

[*She picks up an empty plate from the supper table.*]

IF

JOHN

Madam, I do not know how to thank you.

MARY

O, don't mention it.

JOHN

I have not met such kindness for three years. I . . . I'm starving. I've known better times.

MARY [*kindly*]

I'll get you something. You've known better times, you say?

JOHN

I had been intended for work in the City. And then, then I travelled, and—and I got very much taken with foreign countries, and I thought—but it all went to pieces. I lost everything. Here I am, starving.

MARY [*as one might reply to the Mayoress who had lost her gloves*]

O, I'm so sorry.

[JOHN *sighs deeply.*]

MARY

I'll get a nice bit of something to eat.

IF

JOHN

A thousand thanks to you, madam.

[*Exit* MARY *with the plate.*]

LIZA [*who has been standing near the door all the time*]

Well, she's going to get you something.

JOHN

Heaven reward her.

LIZA

Hungry as all that?

JOHN

I'm on my beam ends.

LIZA

Cheer up!

JOHN

That's all very well to say, living in a fine house, as you are, dry and warm and well-fed. But what have I to cheer up about?

LIZA

Isn't there anything you could pop?

JOHN

What?

LIZA

Nothing you can take to the pawn-shop? I've tided over times I wanted a bit of cash that way sometimes.

IF

JOHN

What could I pawn?

LIZA

Well, well you've a watch-chain.

JOHN

A bit of old leather.

LIZA

But what about the watch?

JOHN

I've no watch.

LIZA

O, funny having a watch-chain then.

JOHN

O, that's only for this; it's a bit of crystal.

LIZA

Funny bit of a thing. What's it for?

JOHN

I don't know.

LIZA

Was it give to you?

JOHN

I don't know. I don't know how I got it.

179

IF

LIZA

Don't know how you got it?

JOHN

No, I can't remember at all. But I've a feeling about it, I can't explain what I feel; but I don't part with it.

LIZA

Don't you? You might get something on it, likely, and have a square meal.

JOHN

I won't part with it.

LIZA

Why?

JOHN

I feel I won't. I never have.

LIZA

Feel you won't?

JOHN

Yes, I have that feeling very strongly. I've kept it always. Everything else is gone.

LIZA

Had it long?

JOHN

Yes, yes. About ten years. I found I had it one morning in a train. It's odd that I can't remember.

IF

LIZA

But wot d'yer keep it for?

JOHN

Just for luck.

[LIZA *breaks into laughter.*]

LIZA

Well, you are funny.

JOHN

I'm on my beam ends. I don't know if that is funny.

LIZA

You're as down in your luck as ever you can be, and you go keeping a thing like that for luck. Why, you couldn't be funnier.

JOHN

Well, what would you do?

LIZA

Why, I 'ad a mascot once, all real gold; and I had rotten luck. Rotten luck I had. Rotten.

JOHN

And what did you do?

LIZA

Took it back to the shop.

JOHN

Yes?

LIZA

They was quite obliging about it. Gave me a wooden one instead, what was guaranteed. Luck changed very soon altogether.

JOHN

Could luck like mine change?

LIZA

Course it could.

JOHN

Look at me.

LIZA

You'll be all right one of these days. Give me that mascot.

JOHN

I—I hardly like to. One has an awfully strong feeling with it.

LIZA

Give it to me. It's no good.

JOHN

I—I don't like to.

IF

LIZA

You just give it to me. I tell you it's doing you no good. I know all about them mascots. Give it me.

JOHN

Well, well, I'll give it you. You're the first woman that's been kind to me since . . . I'm on my beam ends.

[*Face in hands—tears.*]

LIZA

There, there. I'm going to smash it, I am. These mascots! One's better without 'em. Your luck'll turn, never fear. And you've a nice supper coming.

[*She puts it in a corner of the mantelpiece and hammers it. It smashes.*

The photographs of the four children change slightly. The Colonel gives place to Aunt Martha. The green sofa turns red. JOHN's clothes become neat and tidy. The hammer in LIZA's hand turns to a feather duster. Nothing else changes.]

A VOICE [*off, in agony*]

Allah! Allah! Allah!

LIZA

Some foreign gentleman must have hurt himself.

IF

JOHN

H'm. Sounds like it . . . Liza.

[LIZA, *dusting the photographs on the wall, just behind the corner of the mantelpiece.*]

LIZA

Funny. Thought I—thought I 'ad a hammer in my hand.

JOHN

Really, Liza, I often think you have. You really should be more careful. Only—only yesterday you broke the glass of Miss Jane's photograph.

LIZA

Thought it was a hammer.

JOHN

Really, I think it sometimes is. It's a mistake you make too often, Liza. You—you must be more careful.

LIZA

Very well, sir. Funny my thinking I 'ad an 'ammer in my 'and, though.

[She goes to tidy the little supper table. Enter MARY with food on a plate.]

MARY

I've brought you your supper, John.

IF

JOHN

Thanks, Mary. I—I think I must have taken a nap.

MARY

Did you, dear? Thanks, Liza. Run along to bed now, Liza. Good gracious, it's half-past eleven.

[MARY *makes final arrangements of supper table.*]

LIZA

Thank you, mum.

[*Exit.*]

JOHN

Mary.

MARY

Yes, John.

JOHN

I—I thought I'd caught that train.

Curtain

185